Threatened Species

ISSUES

Volume 78

Editor

Craig Donnellan

Independence

First published by Independence
PO Box 295
Cambridge CB1 3XP
England

British Library Cataloguing in Publication Data
Threatened Species – (Issues Series)
I. Donnellan, Craig II. Series
578.6'8

ISBN 1 86168 267 0 ✓

Printed in Great Britain
MWL Print Group Ltd

Typeset by
Claire Boyd

Cover
The illustration on the front cover is by
Pumpkin House.

CONTENTS

Chapter One: The Worldwide Situation

Chapter Two: The UK Situation

Introduction

Threatened Species is the seventy-eighth volume in the **Issues** series. The aim of this series is to offer up-to-date information about important issues in our world.

Threatened Species looks at plants and animals that are under threat, both in the UK and around the world.

The information comes from a wide variety of sources and includes:
Government reports and statistics
Newspaper reports and features
Magazine articles and surveys
Web site material
Literature from lobby groups
and charitable organisations.

It is hoped that, as you read about the many aspects of the issues explored in this book, you will critically evaluate the information presented. It is important that you decide whether you are being presented with facts or opinions. Does the writer give a biased or an unbiased report? If an opinion is being expressed, do you agree with the writer?

Threatened Species offers a useful starting-point for those who need convenient access to information about the many issues involved. However, it is only a starting-point. At the back of the book is a list of organisations which you may want to contact for further information.

*****

Endangered animals of the world

Information from the Young People's Trust for the Environment

Life began on our planet about 3,500 million years ago. The first living things were found in the sea, and over the course of millions of years, from these early life forms, a rich variety of animals has descended. Through the process we call evolution, animals have become adapted to enable them to live in all parts of the world, sometimes in the most hostile environments.

Almost 600 million years ago, the invertebrates appeared, i.e. those animals without backbones – insects and other minibeasts. The earliest vertebrates, i.e. animals with backbones, were in the form of primitive fish and appeared around 500 million years ago. From these, all the other fishes descended, as well as amphibians, reptiles, birds and mammals.

The animal kingdom is enormous and we do not know for certain how many species there are in the world. Around 1.5 million species of animal have been named and described by scientists – and over a million of these are insects. It is known that there are about twice as

many animals in tropical rainforests than in any other habitat, and it is here that there are likely to be countless numbers of species yet unknown to science. It has been estimated that the total number of insect species alone could be around 30 million!

It is just possible, but unlikely, that there are a few large animals remaining to be discovered, but what we can be sure of is that the most numerous large animal on Earth is *Homo sapiens* – the human! Modern man appeared about 30,000 years ago and has increasingly come to dominate the planet. The steady increase in population was speeded up by advances in civilisation such as the Industrial Revolution and better health and medical care.

The rate in increase of the human population is slowing down in parts of the Northern Hemisphere, but it continues to rise in Third World countries, despite the effect of famine, floods, disease and war. Allowing for the deathrate, over one million more humans come into the world each week!

This population explosion means that millions of people suffer from hunger and disease, and more and more wild places are taken over, causing animals and plants to suffer too.

Extinction is for ever!

As almost everyone knows, to become extinct is to be gone for ever. Even before man's arrival on Earth, species became extinct quite naturally. Natural extinction happens when a species declines in numbers gradually but steadily at the end of its evolu-tionary period on Earth. The length of this period depends on how well a species can adapt to changes in climate and changes in other animals and plants around it. This process of extinction can take a very long time – sometimes several million years – and the extinction of one species is immediately followed by the appearance of another in a continuous cycle.

The case of the dinosaurs is the most well-known example of natural extinction. These reptiles appeared on Earth about 200 million years ago and dominated both land and sea for almost 100 million years. It is not certain why the dinosaurs became extinct, but their disappearance was a natural one and new species of animals evolved to replace them.

The rate of extinction has speeded up unnaturally over the last 400 years, rising sharply since 1900.

...TRYING TO FIND SOME SPACE...

This increase in the rate of extinction is directly related to the increase in the human population over the same period of time. The vast number of humans has caused great damage to the planet, as wild habitats have been taken over, forcing animals and plants into smaller and smaller areas, until some of them have become extinct. We have also polluted some habitats with chemicals and refuse, making them unfit for wildlife. These causes of extinction are known as indirect destruction.

Animals may also become extinct through direct destruction. This includes the hunting and capturing of animals. Man has always

Today there are about 5,000 endangered animals and at least one species dies out every year

hunted and killed wildlife but when early humans lived more in harmony with nature, they killed animals for essential food and clothing. When firearms were invented mass destruction of species was possible. Animals have been, and still are, killed for meat, clothing, medicines, feathers, eggs, trophies, tourist souvenirs – and sometimes just for amusement. Some species are still captured in the wild for the live pet trade, even though their numbers are dwindling.

The extinction of at least 500 species of animals has been caused by man, most of them in the last century. Today there are about 5,000 endangered animals and at least one species dies out every year. There are probably many more which become extinct without anyone knowing.

■ The above information is from the Young People's Trust for the Environment's web site: www.yptenc.org.uk
© Young People's Trust for the Environment

Endangered treasures

A total of 16,697 species of plants and animals are included in the International Union for Conservation of Nature and Natural Resources' 2002 Red List of threatened and endangered species. Every one of them has its own specific story. Here are some of the less well-known species at risk

Birds

■ Around 28,000 mature wandering albatross birds (Vulnerable) nest on sub-Antarctic islands and fish across the southern oceans. The main risk to the species stems from long-line fisheries – many birds drown after diving at baited hooks. Like other albatross species, the wandering albatross is undergoing a long-term decline and is listed as vulnerable.

■ The endangered Philippine eagle's population is small and rapidly declining – there may be only 350-650 birds left of an original population of about 6,000. A major threat is loss of old-growth forest habitat. Conservation measures in action include laws against persecution of the birds, protection of nests, survey work, public awareness campaigns, and captive breeding. The eagle's future will only be secured by forest conservation.

Reptiles

■ South Asian box turtles (Threatened) are widespread in fresh waters from Bangladesh to Japan. Eight out of the nine species are now considered threatened, out of which six are critically endangered. The main source of threat is harvesting for the food and traditional medicine market in East Asia. Hundreds of thousands of specimens have been traded over the last decade. Legislation protects some species in some countries, but is often not effectively enforced.

■ The Chinese alligator is one of the world's most endangered crocodilians. It is found in the lower parts of the Yangtze River, in wetland habitats that have dense human populations. The species is very secretive and spends a large part of the year hibernating in burrows. The greatest threats are habitat destruction and killing by local farmers because the alligators' burrows damage farmland. The Chinese government is now developing a conservation plan.

Plants

■ The Alabama canebrake pitcher-plant (Critically Endangered) is found only in central Alabama. Alabama has lost over half its wetlands in the past 200 years, and as a result many wetland species have declined. Major threats include invasive species, herbicide damage, over-collection, and draining of bog habitats. Four of the 12 remaining populations have up to 300 plants, while the rest have no more than 50. Work is under way to try to restore the degraded habitats to their natural state.

■ The red-flowered Mandrinette shrub (Critically Endangered) is found only on two mountains on Mauritius. One population, of some 20 adults, is not regenerating, probably due to competition from introduced species. The second population of 26 plants was recently found at the top of Morne Brabant Mountain in an area degraded by invasive species. The Mandrinette grows well from cuttings and is being artificially propagated. The only hope for its survival is to manage the two known wild populations by weeding out the exotic competitors and artificially restocking the areas when needed.

Land mammals

- The Tibetan antelope (Endangered) lives on the Tibetan Plateau, and small areas of northern India and western Nepal. Their wool is known as 'shahtoosh' or 'king of wool'. Expensive shahtoosh shawls and scarves are now high fashion in the West. The demand has fuelled poaching, and illegal trade thrives, despite conservation and enforcement efforts by the Chinese government. As recently as 40-50 years ago, up to a million Tibetan antelope may have roamed the Plateau, but numbers have been declining rapidly and could now be as low as 65,000-75,000 individuals.
- The fossa (Endangered) is a dog-like carnivore that lives in the rainforests of Madagascar. In 1996, it was listed as vulnerable, but it is now classified as endangered because the total population is estimated to be below 2,500 mature individuals. Numbers are declining due to deforestation and persecution, since the fossa eats small domestic animals.

Primates

- The Cross River gorilla (Critically Endangered) is the most endangered subspecies of gorilla. Populations are found only on densely forested hills on the Nigeria-Cameroon border. The total remaining population may be as few as 150 to 200 individuals, fragmented into five or more clusters. The major threat is hunting for bushmeat. Only one sub-population is officially fully protected, in Nigeria's Cross River National Park. Efforts are under way to protect the remaining animals and to establish a cross-border conservation programme.
- Miss Waldron's red colobus (Critically Endangered) may be the closest to extinction of any primate. Recent surveys have failed to reveal any surviving populations in Côte d'Ivoire and Ghana where it is believed to have lived. However, there is evidence that the animals were being hunted. Primatologists believe that the last refuge may be in forests surrounding the Ehi Lagune in south-eastern Côte d'Ivoire and an expedition is being mounted to locate them. If no evidence is found, this may be the only primate to have become extinct during the 20th century.

Threatened species on the IUCN Red List

	No. of species in group	No. of threatened species in 2002	% of total in group threatened in 2002
Plants	265,876	5,716	2%
Mammals	4,763	1,137	24%
Birds	9,946	1,192	12%
Reptiles	7,970	293	4%
Amphibians	4,950	156	3%
Fish	25,000	742	3%
Invertebrates	1,190,200	1,932	0.2%

Source: IUCN

Sea mammals

- Numbers of sea otters (Endangered) have dropped by 90 per cent in western Alaska, and there have been significant declines in California and the Russian Federation. The species occurs along the northern Pacific coast, from northern Japan, to California. Threats include oil pollution, frequent poaching, and conflicts with fisheries.
- Hector's dolphin (Endangered) is found only in New Zealand waters and the population is fragmented. The main threat is entanglement in gillnets. Additional threats include disease, habitat modification, and

deaths through collisions with vessels. Hector's dolphins also accumulate toxic chemicals including DDT, PCBs, and dioxins. To date, only one sanctuary has been created around Banks Peninsula.

Fish

- The common sawfish (Critically Endangered) was once common in the Mediterranean and eastern Atlantic, but it has been eliminated from Europe and the Mediterranean. Its status in West Africa is unknown, but it is believed to be severely depleted in areas where shark fisheries have increased production. Without timely intervention, it is likely that this sawfish will become extinct.
- The Brazilian guitarfish (Critically Endangered) is a species of ray found along the coast of southern Brazil. Its numbers fell by 96 per cent between 1984 and 1994 through over-fishing. Fishers catch juveniles two to three years before they reach maturity. The fishery is not solely dependent on the Brazilian guitarfish, so its near-extinction will not cause the fishery to close. It is therefore likely that this guitarfish could be driven to extinction in the near future.

- The above information is from *People & the Planet*'s web site: www.peopleandplanet.net

© *People & the Planet* 2000-2003

Return of the great white hunters

Wealthy Britons pay tens of thousands to bag a lion, elephant or polar bear in trophy hunts that recreate images of a bygone colonial era

It is an image of a bygone era: the colonial hunter sitting atop an elephant in the Indian jungle preparing to shoot a tiger or any other large creature that happens to wander into his gun-sights.

But an investigation into the growing trade of trophy hunting reveals that record numbers of wealthy British hunters are paying £10,000 or more for the privilege of slaughtering big game in Africa, North America and Eastern Europe

Leopards, cheetahs, elephants, hippos and polar bears are being killed in unprecedented numbers. Many of them are among the most threatened species on the planet, yet there has been a fourfold increase in hunting trophies being imported into the UK since 1998. Conservationists and animal rights groups fear that the increase is pushing some species close to extinction.

One reason for the growth in popularity of trophy-hunting trips is that they are increasingly easy to arrange over the internet. An *Observer* reporter posing as a customer contacted several hunting outfits and was offered the chance to kill lions in Tanzania, elephants in Botswana, cheetahs in Zimbabwe, polar bears in Canada and grizzly bears in Russia.

The largest organiser in the UK is Holland and Holland, the royal gunsmith based in Mayfair and best known for supplying guns to the Duke of Edinburgh and the Prince of Wales. It has also supplied shotguns to celebrities such as Madonna and her husband, Guy Ritchie.

Piers Vaux, director of Holland and Holland's sporting department, offered the reporter a 14-day hunt in Zimbabwe at its 'luxurious camps' on the banks of the Zambezi, where he would be able to shoot elephants and cheetahs. The cost would be

By Antony Barnett, Public Affairs Editor

$24,250, which included the cost of one elephant trophy at $10,000.

Vaux assured the reporter that the political turmoil in Zimbabwe was no problem, but did recommend that Botswana was the best place for killing elephants.

'Last year we had the second best area for elephants in the country and this year we are due to be the first,' he said. 'Botswana is producing the largest elephants in Africa. These statistics point us in the direction of being one of the best areas in the continent for elephants.'

> *One reason for the growth in popularity of trophy-hunting trips is that they are increasingly easy to arrange over the internet*

Vaux quoted a price of $47,200 for a two-week hunt in the Okavango delta in Botswana. He confirmed that he was sending more 'English' hunters than ever out to Africa and believed it was because people are becoming 'more adventurous'. He described how once the animals are killed they are sent to a taxidermist in South Africa, where they are stuffed, mounted and then sent to the UK.

Hendry Ramsay & Waters, a Scottish operator, told the reporter he could arrange a lion or leopard hunt in Tanzania for £10,000.

British operators point out they act strictly within the law and take

part only in licensed hunts approved by international authorities. They argue that their hunts pose no threats to endangered animal populations and aid the environment by bringing much-needed revenue into impoverished communities.

Yet last week a report by the Wildlife Conservation Research Unit at Oxford University warned that the number of African lions being shot must be radically cut if the species is to survive. Others also believe that the large amounts of foreign money pouring into trophy hunting leaves the system of licensed kills open to abuse.

According to figures prepared for *The Observer* by the World Conservation Monitoring Centre – an agency of the United Nations Environment Programme – 44 potentially endangered animals were killed last year by British hunters and brought back to the UK as trophy heads. In 1998, only 10 suffered this fate.

The latest trophies include 13 leopards, seven grizzly bears, six cheetahs, five polar bears, four hippos and three African elephants. The populations of these animals have fallen dramatically over the decades and they are listed as vulnerable by the Convention on International Trade in Endangered Species.

Research has shown that removing just a single lion from a population could lead to a drastic fall in numbers. It is estimated that there are only 23,000 lions in Africa, about one-tenth of what some suggest there were in 1980. Similar fears of extinction exist for the leopard population. Figures obtained by *The Observer* show that, between 2001 and 2002, British hunters killed four lions and 23 leopards in such places as South Africa, Namibia, Tanzania and Zimbabwe.

Despite the pull of Africa, one of the most popular destinations for British hunters is the North-West Territories of Canada, where polar bears can be hunted for about $25,000 a time. In the past two years, they have killed 15 polar bears and brought their trophies back to the UK. Although there are no British operators offering such trips, the internet means it is easy to book one by computer. One US outfit, Four Star Hunting, provides the 'ultimate global hunting destinations for the discriminating hunter'. Its website offers the chance for a hunter to kill almost any animal anywhere in the world and bring a trophy home.

One of its consultants, Ron Simmons, offered a polar-bear hunt for $22,500 and said he had a client from England 'who hunted polar bears with me last season and took a very good bear'. Another operator, Adventure North West, shows on its website a collection of polar bears and other species its clients have killed. US operators claim these are regulated hunts which benefit the Inuit community.

Animal rights groups have expressed revulsion at the number of

Britons killing vulnerable mammals for sport. Douglas Batchelor, chief executive of the League Against Cruel Sports, said: 'We find it shocking that it is legal for trophy hunters to be allowed to travel abroad to shoot and import the body parts of rare and endangered species to adorn their boardrooms and country-house retreats.'

Conservationists are particularly worried about the number of grizzly bears being killed in British Columbia in Canada, where they believe the species is being pushed close to extinction.

Wendy Elliott, a campaigner for the Environmental Investigation Agency, said: 'Concerns have been raised for decades by scientists that the grizzly-bear hunt in British Columbia is unsustainable and is pushing the population into a possibly irreversible decline. We are in danger of returning to the policies of the imperial age, with the great white hunter contributing to the decline of some of our planet's most enigmatic species.'

Until recently, trophy hunting has mainly been the preserve of wealthy Americans and Germans hoping to follow in the footsteps of Ernest Hemingway. But although the rise in the number of British hunters taking part in these trips has surprised some, others link it to the potential ban on foxhunting in the UK.

'It will come as no surprise if foreign trophy hunting becomes the sport of choice for those facing a ban on hunting with hounds and similar pursuits in the UK,' Batchelor said. 'Hunters who are rich enough will look for their thrills elsewhere. The only solution is for the EU to ban imports of trophy parts of animals killed for sport.'

■ This article first appeared in *The Observer*, 12 October 2003.
© Guardian Newspapers Limited 2003

Wonderful wildlife

Information from Animal Aid

Endangered species

It is thought that there are about 10 million different species of plants and animals in the world, although only 2 million have been recorded so far.

Many could soon become extinct because of the selfish activities of one species – man. Why are so many animals in danger?

Habitat destruction

The tropical rainforest is the world's richest natural habitat. Over two-thirds of all the plant and animal species on earth live there. Sadly it is being rapidly destroyed – half has already gone – cut down for timber and cleared to make room for farm land. If the rainforest disappears, then all the plants and animals that live there will be lost for ever.

Among those threatened is the Central African gorilla. Despite their gentle, harmless nature, these creatures have been feared and persecuted by man for centuries. Of the three sub-species, the mountain gorilla is the most endangered. There are thought to be only 700 of these amazing creatures left in Uganda, Rwanda and Zaire.

Pandas live in the bamboo forests of China which are also being destroyed to make way for a rapidly growing human population. Many years ago, pandas were found all over China; now there are just 1,000 or so, left high up in the mountains in the south-west of the country. Efforts to save the panda bear have concentrated on creating reserves and trying to protect the little bit of forest habitat that remains.

Hunting

The tiger is just one of many species of wild cats that now face extinction because of hunting and habitat loss. At the beginning of this century over 100,000 tigers roamed across much of Asia, from Turkey to India and Siberia. Today it is estimated that there are fewer than 5,000 tigers left. Already three of the eight sub-species (the Bali, Caspian and Javanese tigers) are extinct. There are thought to be only 200 Siberian tigers left and the South China tiger may already be down to single figures.

In the past tigers were hunted for their skins and for sport. Today they are hunted because virtually all their body parts, including bones, eyes and whiskers, are used in oriental medicines. Many of the countries where tigers live have recently signed up to the conservation agreement known as CITES and have agreed to ban the trade in tiger products. Enforcing the laws, however, is difficult because the criminals who kill tigers and trade in their body parts make a lot of money.

CITES (the Convention on International Trade in Endangered Species) is a United Nations agreement that protects endangered species by regulating or banning the trade in wild animals and animal products. The trouble is that not every country belongs to CITES and even many of those countries who have signed up to the treaty don't enforce it properly.

Whales have been ruthlessly hunted for centuries and, as a result, several species have been driven almost to extinction. In 1982, the International Whaling Commission (IWC) voted for a moratorium (ban) on all commercial whaling starting in 1985. Norway and Japan, however, continue to kill some whales because of the loop-hole allowing whales to be killed for so-called 'scientific research'.

Rhinos have roamed the earth for over 40 million years but soon they could be extinct because of man's greed. The world population of all five species is now less than 10,500 animals. The number of African black rhinos has crashed from 100,000 animals in 1960 to less than 2,500 and there are now only 80 Javan rhinos left. Rhinos are killed for their horn which is ground up and used as an ingredient in traditional Asian medicines. This is despite a CITES ban on the trade.

The African elephant, the world's largest land animal, also faces extinction. A century ago there were 10 million; 10 years ago there were 1 million; but today there are only

---

Rhinos have roamed the earth for over 40 million years but soon they could be extinct because of man's greed

---

about 500,000 left. Elephants are killed for their ivory tusks, which are made into trivial trinkets and jewellery. In 1989 CITES banned the sale of ivory and other elephant products. This was a major conservation breakthrough and has meant that far fewer elephants are now being shot. But as the human population in Africa grows there is less room for elephants. This has meant that some African countries have started selectively killing (or culling) elephants in their game parks to keep their numbers down.

Pollution

Many of the world's wild animals are threatened by the pollution which results from man's industrial and farming activities. It is thought that 150,000 different chemicals (including heavy metals, pesticides and industrial waste) are dumped and washed into the sea every year. The animals who live in the oceans, particularly those at the ends of the food chains, absorb these poisonous chemicals. For example, the bodies of seals, whales, dolphins and even Arctic polar bears have been found to contain high levels of PCBs, a material which could destroy the animals' ability to reproduce. It is

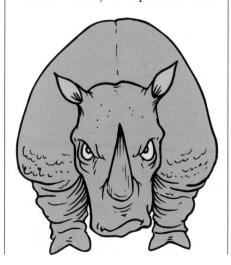

now thought that chemical pollution in the sea poses as great a threat to the survival of whales as the whaling fleets did in the past.

Urban development

In Britain today lots of wild animals such as wild cats, pine martens, otters, sand lizards and red kites are facing extinction. Their habitats are threatened because of urban development and modern intensive farming practices. The 'improvement' of farm land, the building of roads, factories, houses, shops and leisure facilities all take up more and more space, which means fewer woods, ponds, hedges, meadows, moorlands and other open wild spaces for wild animals to live in.

Why does it matter?

Some people say that we should conserve animals and plants because they might be useful to us in the future. Others say that in the long term, our own survival may depend on maintaining the planet's ecosystems. This means preserving other species and maintaining the planet's 'biodiversity' (or variety of life). Animal Aid believes, quite simply, that we have a responsibility to protect animals for their own sake and especially to protect those species which our own actions and greed have endangered.

A recent United Nations report estimated that nearly half of all birds and mammals will be extinct within 300 years.

Solutions

■ Conserve the world's natural habitats. Protecting individual species in zoos is not a solution. Only through protection of their habitats will wild animals survive.

■ Ban the international trade in products made from endangered species and enforce the laws that protect wild animals.

■ Educate people so that they stop buying animal products.

■ Stop polluting the environment with poisonous wastes.

■ The above information is from Animal Aid's web site which can be found at www.animalaid.org.uk

Half of the world's plant species 'under threat'

By Roger Highfield,
Science Editor

Scientists have seriously under-estimated the extent to which the world's flora is threatened with extinction, with up to half of all species now thought to be under threat.

The very existence of life on Earth depends upon plants – not just on sheer numbers but also on the diversity of species, currently estimated at between 310,000 and 422,000.

Previous estimates of threatened plants – up to 13 per cent – did not include a reliable tally of species at risk in the tropical latitudes, where most of the world's plants grow, according to Dr Nigel Pitman, of Duke University, North Carolina, and Dr Peter Jorgensen, of Missouri Botanical Garden in St Louis.

They estimated the missing tropical data using the number of plant species that are endemic to a country, which they say is a reasonable proxy, given that 91 per cent of threatened species in the most comprehensive study to date are endemic to a single country. While these data are not perfect, they are consistently better than data on threatened species, they reported in the journal *Science*.

Using the data for 189 countries and territories, the authors calculated that the global percentage of threatened plants is between 22 and 47 per cent. The Royal Botanic Gardens, Kew, has launched a Threatened Plants Appeal to secure the future of the world's most threatened species by repatriating or reintroducing them to protected areas.

Madagascar is a particular worry. Around 80 per cent of its flora is unique, yet most of that original plant life will disappear within two decades unless action is taken.

Work is in progress to re-introduce the Chilean blue crocus (*Tecophilea cyanocrocus*) to its native Chile, and the toromiro tree (*Sophoro toromiro*) to Easter Island. The appeal also includes British native species such as the cornflower (*Centaurea cyanus*) which, as a result of changes in farming practices, is now endangered.

Among other species under threat worldwide are:

Mandrinette (*Hibiscus fragilis*), found in Mauritius in the Indian Ocean. There are only 46 mature plants left at the two known localities under threat from introduced plant species.

The Bastard Quiver Tree (*Aloe pillansii*) is found in the mountainous Richtersveld area of the Northern Cape, South Africa, and southern Namibia. A decline in the population has reduced the numbers to fewer than 200 mature individuals.

> *The very existence of life on Earth depends upon plants – not just on sheer numbers but also on the diversity of species*

Golden Pagoda (*Mimetes chrysanthus*) was only discovered in 1987. Since that time, a number of small sub-populations have been found along the mountain ranges bordering the Little Karoo, Western Cape, South Africa. The main sub-population is in a nature reserve, however, frequent wild fires and invasive alien species pose a constant threat to this species.

Rabo-De-Raposa (*Micrantho-cereus auriazureus*) is an endangered Brazilian cactus which is threatened by future flooding as a result of dam construction in the area.

Bulbophyllum hamelinii. First described by the Kew orchid grower William Watson in 1893, this plant has rarely been seen since. It is distinguished by its large flowers whose scent and colour resemble rotting flesh. It grows as an epiphyte in humid Madagascan rainforest that is being rapidly deforested.

Biznaguita (*Mammillaria sanchez-mejoradae*), found in a single area in Mexico, has fallen in numbers by 75 per cent over 15 years so there are now fewer than 500 plants.

Trochetia parviflora. Thought extinct for the past 138 years until it was rediscovered in April last year on a Mauritian mountainside. Since then, another 62 plants have been found but it is vulnerable to fire and landslides.

© Telegraph Group Limited, London 2003

Globally threatened birds

Information from BirdLife International

How serious is the situation?

One in eight bird species is globally threatened . . .

BirdLife's latest research shows that a shocking 1,186 bird species (12% of the total or one in eight) are globally threatened with extinction. Of these, 182 bird species are judged to be Critically Endangered (meaning that they are considered to be facing an extremely high risk of extinction), a further 321 are Endangered (very high risk of extinction) and 680 are Vulnerable (high risk of extinction). An additional 727 (Near Threatened) species are assessed as close to qualifying as globally threatened.

. . . because of declines . . .

Even numerous and widespread birds may be threatened owing to rapidly declining populations. Species are considered globally threatened if continued declines would result in their extinction within 100 years. Overall, there are 425 Globally Threatened Birds (36% of the total) with populations declining at these rates.

. . . small populations . . .

Most Globally Threatened Birds are threatened because they have small populations. There are 961 species (81% of the total) with populations of fewer than 10,000 mature individuals and 78% of these are also declining.

. . . or small ranges

Small range is also an important threat factor. There are 856 Globally Threatened Birds (72% of the total) with ranges smaller than 20,000 km². Of these, 70% are undergoing declines in numbers, range or available habitat.

Hundreds of bird species could become extinct . . .

Extinction is a natural process. The fossil record indicates that, without human influence, we might expect one bird species to die out every 100 years or so. But BirdLife has documented the extinction of 128 bird species since 1500, with 103 of these since 1800. This is more than 50 times the background rate. BirdLife now predicts that over 460 Globally Threatened Birds could become extinct by 2100 if current trends continue. This is nearly 500 times the background rate.

. . . indicating major changes to the earth's ecosystems

Species extinctions are no longer occasional natural events but the result of major changes to the earth's ecosystems. These same systems provide vital services – such as maintaining global climate patterns, safeguarding watersheds and stabilising soils – for all biodiversity, including people. They must be safeguarded for future generations.

Why is there a problem?

Habitat loss is the most serious issue . . .

Over 1,000 Globally Threatened Birds (85% of the total) are affected by habitat loss and degradation, indicating that this is the most serious

> ### Case study: Nukupu'u
>
> The Nukupu'u, a honeyeater from the Hawaiian Islands classified as Critically Endangered, is on the verge of extinction owing to a multitude of threats. For example, agricultural activities such as cattle ranching have nearly destroyed all lowland forests, while introduced ungulates have degraded montane forests and feral pigs have spread alien plants and disease-carrying mosquitoes. Periodic hurricanes may be the ultimate cause of its extinction, despite intensive conservation efforts.

issue impacting biodiversity. Some 540 Globally Threatened Birds (46% of the total) are at particular risk of extinction owing to severe fragmentation of their habitat and isolation in a few locations. Species that were once widespread are affected, as well as those with naturally confined ranges (e.g. on islands or mountains).

. . . most commonly caused by agricultural expansion . . .

The main driving force leading to habitat loss and degradation is agricultural expansion. Over 800 Globally Threatened Birds (nearly 70% of the total) are affected by, for example, plantations, arable and livestock farming, and smallholder and shifting agriculture. The widespread conversion of natural forest to commercial plantations (e.g. oil palm, rubber and tea) is a particular concern. These cultivated 'monocultures' are usually of little or no importance for conservation.

. . . and extraction of natural resources

Other significant driving forces leading to habitat loss and degradation are the extraction of natural resources (notably for timber products) and infrastructure development (such as road building, human settlements and industry). Nearly 600 Globally Threatened Birds (>50% of the total) and over 350 Globally Threatened Birds (c.30% of the total) are affected respectively.

Hunting and trade are also important . . .

Over 350 Globally Threatened Birds (c.30% of the total) are affected by exploitation for human use, primarily through hunting for food (>200 species) and trapping for the cagebird trade (>100 species).

. . . as are invasive species . . .

Over 350 Globally Threatened Birds (c.30% of the total), many of which are confined to islands, are impacted by invasive species. In most cases these are introduced predators such as cats, rats and mongooses. Invasive species have been a major factor in most bird extinctions since 1800, so this is a particular concern.

...with climate change a looming problem

Studies show that global warming is already having measurable effects on habitats, and the ranges and behaviour of some bird species. At present, relatively few Globally Threatened Birds are known to be directly affected by climate change. Most of these are seabirds, where oceanic warming is associated with food shortages. As climate change accelerates owing to atmospheric pollution, it is predicted that it will become a major problem for many species, often exacerbating the impacts of habitat loss and fragmentation.

Many threats are also interconnected

Many bird species are at risk from multiple threats. For example, nearly 90% of those species affected by timber extraction also suffer from the conversion of these lands to plantations or other agricultural practices; and 70% of those species affected by direct exploitation also suffer from habitat loss.

Case study: Wandering Albatross

The Wandering Albatross, classified as Vulnerable, is highly susceptible to being drowned after striking at the baited hooks of longline fishing boats. It breeds on Macquarie Island (Australia), South Georgia (to UK), Crozet and Kerguelen Islands (French Southern Territories) and Prince Edward and Marion Islands (South Africa), dispersing widely in all the southern oceans. Although it is still quite numerous (some 28,000 individuals), data from two breeding sites indicate severe declines. The impact of incidental bycatch of seabirds in the fisheries is rising, with the number of albatross and petrel species classed as globally threatened increasing from 32 to 55 between 1994 and 2000.

Can threatened birds be saved?

Sound information can conserve birds...

BirdLife's extensive documentation of the status of the 1,186 Globally Threatened Birds has enabled nearly 5,500 key actions to be identified. Carrying them out will significantly enhance the status of the world's birds.

...with concerted effort...

Globally Threatened Birds will only be conserved through the concerted effort of local people, non-governmental organisations, government departments and the private sector working together in partnership.

...even those on the brink of extinction

With focused effort it is possible to save species even on the very brink of extinction. The Seychelles Warbler, for example, has undergone a spectacular recovery. In 1959, 30 birds were counted and in 1965 it was estimated that about 50 adults were present on the tiny island of Cousin. In 1968, BirdLife purchased Cousin and, following an intensive management and translocation programme, the species is now secure, with a population of more than 2,000 birds spread over three islands.

We must act now...

We must act now to prevent more bird species becoming threatened, and to save the 182 species judged to be Critically Endangered. They are facing an extremely high risk of extinction in the immediate future, perhaps as high as 50% in 10 years. Nearly 30 of these species may already be extinct – they have not been recorded for at least five years and, in

some cases, for over 100 years, but exhaustive surveys are needed to confirm their status and conservation needs.

...monitor our efforts...

Monitoring programmes are needed to determine trends in the populations of bird species, the pressures they face, and the responses undertaken. Such monitoring will provide an early warning of sudden changes so that appropriate action can be taken.

Case study: Seychelles Magpie-robin

The Seychelles Magpie-robin was once found on at least six islands in the Seychelles, but by 1965 the population was reduced to only 12-15 birds on one island, Frégate, as a result of predation by cats and rats, compounded by competition with introduced Common Mynahs, habitat changes and pesticide use. A highly successful recovery programme, initiated in 1990, has involved translocations to small, predator-free islands, and boosting nesting success by habitat creation, supplementary feeding, nest defence, provision of nest boxes, and reduction of competitors. By 2002, the population had grown to 115 individuals on four islands, and the aim is to increase this to >200 individuals on seven islands by 2006, resulting in a downlisting of its status from Critically Endangered to Endangered.

...and evaluate our success

Will the actions under way and planned succeed in stemming the predicted extinction crisis? It is too early to say, and we must continue to evaluate our success. Our effectiveness at conserving the world's birds will indicate our success in safeguarding ecosystem functions and biodiversity as a whole.

■ The above information is an extract from *Globally Threatened Birds – indicating priorities for action*, a publication from BirdLife International. See page 41 for their address details.

© BirdLife International

Unprecedented extinction rate, and it's increasing

By Simon Stuart, IUCN's Head of Species Survival Programme

The world's species face an unprecedented crisis. The rate at which they are being lost is alarming, even when compared with the extinction episode of 70 million years ago when the dinosaurs disappeared. No one knows exactly what the current extinction rate is, but recent calculations by leading scientists put it at between 1,000 and 10,000 times greater than it would naturally be. The rate of extinction also appears to be increasing. Species are threatened in every habitat on every continent, though the severity of threat varies from place to place. Evidence suggests that freshwater habitats, particularly rivers, and oceanic islands are very severely affected by species extinction. Tropical Asia and Australia appear to suffer particularly high extinction rates.

Some of the wealthier parts of the world have been successful in bringing about the recovery of certain species and greater efforts have been made to curb the loss of species over the past 20 years. Yet despite some isolated successes, conservation progress has generally been too little, too late, and the global situation continues to worsen.

There are many causes of the current extinction crisis, but all of them stem from unsustainable management of the planet by humans. Despite efforts to conserve key habitats for animal and plant species, widespread destruction of important habitats continues unchecked. Perhaps even more serious, the quality of habitats continues to deteriorate as a result of harmful activities such as overgrazing, selective logging, removal of dead wood, and burning.

A rapidly growing threat, and one which is very hard to control, is the spread of alien, invasive species. These species, both animals and plants, spread to areas and habitats where they do not naturally occur, displacing native species through predation, competition, disease and hybridisation. People move thousands of alien species around the globe, either deliberately or accidentally. Other species become established outside their natural range by taking advantage of new habitats modified by humans.

Over-harvesting of species, both animals and plants, that are valuable, either for economic or cultural reasons is another universal threat. Such harvests can be intentional (such as timber harvesting, the ivory trade or the pet trade) or unintentional (such as by-catch – the capture of non-target species in fisheries). Many species now appear to be suffering serious declines as a result of climate change, yet the full effects of the problem are little understood. The list of threats goes on – pollution, freak weather events, and disease can all have devastating

The world's rarest mammals

Mammal species with published estimates of worldwide population about 1,000 animals or less (animals are listed in the order of their population estimates, with the rarest first)

• Baiji (Yangtze River Dolphin) . . . only a few tens of individuals	• Hirola (Hunter's Hartebeest) . . . by 1995 numbers were down to 300
• Vancouver Island Marmot . . . at least 24	• African Wild Ass . . . possibly only a few hundred animals
• Seychelles Sheath-tailed Bat . . . fewer than 50 individuals	• Addax . . . may not exceed a few hundred individuals
• Javan Rhino . . . fewer than 60	• Black-faced Lion Tamarin . . . as few as 400
• Hispid Hare (Assam Rabbit) . . . 110	• Ethiopian Wolf . . . 442-487
• Northern Hairy-nosed Wombat . . . 113	• Vaquita . . . about 500
• Tamaraw (Dwarf Water Buffalo) . . . the total population is thought to be about 30-200	• Arabian Oryx . . . approximately 500 animals in the wild
• Dwarf Blue Sheep . . . approximately 200	• Mediterranean Monk Seal . . . only 600 monk seals survive in the mediterrean
• Tonkin Snub-nosed Monkey . . . about 200	• Hairy-eared Dwarf Lemur . . . estimated to number between 100-1000
• Yellow-tailed Woolly Monkey . . . fewer than 250 individuals	
• Kouprey (Cambodian Forest Ox) . . . generally assumed to be less than 250	• Riverine Rabbit . . . the actual population is probably well below 1,000 animals
• Malabar Large Spotted Civet . . . fewer than 250 mature individuals are thought to survive	• Muriqui (Woolly Spider Monkey) . . . 700-1,000
• Sumatran Rhino . . . fewer than 300	• Giant Panda . . . about 1,000
• Iberian Lynx . . . 150-300	• Golden Lion Tamarin . . . 1,000
• Visayan Spotted Deer . . . a few hundred	• Golden Bamboo Lemur . . . about 1,000 individuals
• Indus River Dolphin . . . hundreds	• Golden-rumped Lion Tamarin . . . 1,000
• Saola (Vu Quang Ox) . . . estimated at several hundred	• Greater Bamboo Lemur . . . 1,000 individuals

Source: Animal Info

effects. When species decline so that only very small populations survive, additional, biological factors begin to operate against them. These can include reduced genetic health of the population, and reduced reproductive success.

Presenting a full catalogue of the threats to species can be a depressing task but it should be noted that relatively few of these threats are intentional, or are specific to a particular species. Most relate to large-scale modifications of the Earth's surface by humans, and the loss of species is largely an unintended by-product of the way people have chosen to live. Behind the threats are powerful driving forces that push species to extinction at an increasing rate. For instance, the increasing economic wealth of much of the world is making demands on the natural environment that cannot be met, leading to habitat destruction, over-harvesting of animals and plants, pollution, and climate change. At the opposite end of the spectrum, in the poorer regions of the world, poverty is forcing people to adopt modes of subsistence living involving activities such as burning and over-grazing that are destroying critical habitats for species. The trend to increasing economic globalisation and the relaxation of trade controls lie behind the uncontrolled spread of invasive species.

Species are threatened in every habitat on every continent, though the severity of threat varies from place to place

---

There have been some successes in species conservation over the last 20 years. The decline of the black rhinoceros has been halted, and the species is slowly recovering. The unsustainable trade in certain parrot species has stopped. Several crocodile populations are now well managed and increasing through carefully regulated, sustainable harvesting programmes. In some places, species have been re-introduced to parts of their former range, and are

increasing, such as the Arabian oryx in Jordan. However, these are only isolated examples and such successes are generally achieved through large investments that tackle immediate threats. There have been very few attempts to address the underlying driving forces of species loss.

For the species extinction crisis to be addressed effectively, far greater action is needed, aimed at both the immediate threats to species and the driving forces causing their decline. Addressing these forces will be particularly challenging, because it raises questions about the sustainability of human lifestyles.

These issues will only be tackled if there is much greater support for lifestyle changes, and this involves the political will of governments. Although the world is slowly beginning to address sustainability issues, it is sobering to remember that vast levels of investment and action are needed simply to stop the rate of extinction increasing, let alone bring it under control.

■ The above information is from IUCN's web site which can be found at www.iucn.org
©IUCN International Union for Conservation of Nature and Natural Resources

Disappearing forests

atural forests all over the world are being destroyed by human activities.

Rainforests

Rainforests are found in the tropics of Latin America, Africa and Asia. They play an important part in:
■ regulating the climate
■ stabilising soil and preventing soil erosion
■ storing and purifying water

Rainforests are also home to an incredible amount of biodiversity, including many endangered species like the orang-utan, Sumatran tiger and scarlet macaw parrot.

Did you know?

A single acre of rainforest can contain as many different plant species as the whole of the UK (around 1,500).

Despite their importance for biodiversity and ecosystems, we are destroying forests at an unprecedented rate.

Every year an area of rainforest the size of England is cut down.

Some of the main causes of rainforest destruction are:
■ Logging
   Many trees are unsustainably and even illegally logged to provide timber and pulp for paper.
■ Plantations and cash crops
   Forests are cut down and replaced by plantations of acacia, eucalyptus, palm oil and soya beans.
■ Urbanisation and construction projects
   Expanding cities, new roads, dams and mines eat into the forest. Human rights abuses are also commonplace as companies move in to extract wealth from areas of forest traditionally inhabited by tribal communities.

And elsewhere . . ?

It's not just the rainforests that are under threat. For example, just five per cent of Finland and Sweden's ancient forests (snowforests) remain. The rest have been converted into plantations.

■ The above information is from Friends of the Earth's web site which can be found at www.foe.co.uk

© *Friends of the Earth*

Threatened trees

Wild forests 'living museums' of virtually extinct species

Forests in Chile, made world famous by the series *Walking with Dinosaurs*, have been almost destroyed by fire, killing Monkey Puzzle trees up to 2,000 years old.

This ecological disaster has been brought to international attention by researchers at UNEP World Conservation Monitoring Centre (UNEP-WCMC), Cambridge. Groundbreaking work by Chevening Scholar Cristian Echeverría, based at the Centre, has revealed how fragmentation of wild forests is threatening the extinction of the charismatic Monkey Puzzle tree (*Araucaria araucana*) beloved by Victorian gardeners.

The Monkey Puzzle is among 8,000 tree species under threat of extinction in the wild. It is one of only a handful for which a conservation plan exists. Environmental organisations FFI (Fauna & Flora International) and UNEP-WCMC are collaborating on the Global Trees Campaign which aims to establish the management plans vital for the creation of sustainable forests. An important element of this is the development of a mapping programme leading to a proposed World Atlas of Threatened Trees.

The Department for Environment, Food and Rural Affairs (Defra) are sponsors of a report *Towards a Global Tree Conservation Atlas*, which high-lights the plight of five 'flagship' species which the Global Trees Campaign is working hard to save. Mark Collins, Director of UNEP-WCMC, is grateful for the support of Defra and Elliot Morley, Minister for the Environment and Agri-environment.

Mark Collins is concerned that the future of wild forests has worsened since the Centre published the first global assessment, the 'World List of Threatened Trees' 5 years ago. It showed that over 8, 000 tree species are facing extinction in the wild, with 976 in a critical situation. He comments: 'New research, such as

that on the Monkey Puzzle, is revealing that fragmentation of wild forest and the re-plantation with potentially invasive foreign species are major threats, demonstrating the urgency of managing forests sustainably.'

Professor Peter Ashton of Harvard and the Royal Botanic Gardens, Kew, supports his concerns: 'In the tropics many rare tree species are already functionally extinct. The high diversity of plants in tropical rainforests means that specimens are naturally widely spaced, if forest cover is further fragmented then the probability of a pollinator being within range decreases. Some forests are becoming living museums.'

Mark Collins comments that surprisingly little is known about the status and distribution of tree species, including important timber species such as mahogany: 'Our initial report demonstrates that conservation assessments are required for plant conservation targets to be achieved by 2010. In particular we need spatial data, which will help us to identify the most crucial areas for tree conservation and ensure that these ecoregions are managed effectively to provide the protection required.'

UNEP-WCMC and FFI are seeking public and private sector funding for a proposed 'World Atlas of Threatened Trees', which will provide photographs of the species, full colour maps showing their distribution and status reports compiled by workers in the field and an analysis of policy options to prevent extinctions.

Mark Rose, Executive Director of FFI, believes that further regulation of the timber trade is also required: 'We estimate that almost 50 per cent of the tropical timber in international trade has been illegally logged. 1,000 globally threatened trees are threatened in part by unsustainable levels of felling. Accurate, objective information is required to strengthen international trade control mechanisms such as CITES.'

The report *Towards a Global Tree Conservation Atlas* provides new information about flagship species such as *Araucaria araucana* (Monkey Puzzle), *Swietenia macro-phylla* (Brazilian Mahogany), *Cinnamomum cebuense* (Cebu Cinnamon), *Baillonella toxisperma* (Moabi used for decorative timber, animal feed and cosmetics), *Caesalpinia echinata*, (Pau Brazil, national tree of Brazil).

Defra is funding a conservation programme for the Monkey Puzzle under its Flagship Species Fund which includes the development of a nursery with indigenous people to establish cultivation techniques. These endemic evergreen conifer species may reach 2m in diameter, 50m in height and live over 1,500 years. They also take over 200 years to reach seed-bearing maturity. Cristian Echeverría delivered the first progress report on the project in August 2003.

■ The above information is from UNEP's web site which can be found at www.unep-wcmc.org

Whale watching

A future for whales?

Introduction

Whale watching is booming. Hundreds of thousands of tourists each year are now willing to pay for the privilege of seeing whales, dolphins and porpoises from boats, planes and from the land. But whale watching gives more than just pleasure. Whale watching now brings money into local economies, provides important scientific data, educates the public about conservation and is a viable alternative to whaling.

From whaling . . .

Whales have fascinated humans for thousands of years. They form an integral part of the legends of many indigenous people who both relied on them for food and worshipped them.

By the 11th century, whaling had become a commercial enterprise. Spanish whalers were later joined by whaling fleets from Holland, England and the American colonies. However, whaling reached unsustainable proportions by the 19th century. Explosive harpoon-grenades and factory ships made it possible to catch more whales in four decades of the 19th century than in the previous four centuries.

By the 20th century many whale populations were seriously depleted. Although the International Whaling Commission (IWC), an international body for the regulation and control of whaling, issued a global moratorium on commercial whaling in 1986, whales are still being caught commercially. Japan continues to catch hundreds of whales annually

---

Watching whales can be a breath-taking experience. But it is also a way to educate people about whales and conservation in general

---

(many in the Southern Ocean, designated by the member states as an IWC whale sanctuary), exploiting a loophole for 'scientific research', and sells the meat commercially in Japan. Norway conducts an openly commercial hunt under a legal objection to the moratorium.

To whale watching . . .

Watching whales can be a breath-taking experience. But it is also a way to educate people about whales and conservation in general. Whale-watching guides also provide vital observation data on whales and whale behaviour and contribute to whale research. Most importantly of all, perhaps, whale watching is a commercially viable business and offers a real alternative to whaling. It can give local communities new life through jobs in whale-watching ventures and in related tourism businesses such as restaurants, shops, hotels and guesthouses.

Whale-watching numbers

Until the 1980s, only a few thousand people went whale watching. Their numbers had increased, however, to four million by 1991. By the end of the century, there were more than nine million whale watchers worldwide with 87 countries offering whale-watching tours, and about 500 communities and cities involved in whale-watching programmes. More than one billion US$ a year is now generated by commercial whale watching.

Taiwan, Spain, Italy and Japan have all seen major increases in whale watching. But Iceland has seen the biggest increase in whale-watching visitors in recent years. Whale watching is Iceland's fastest-growing tourism sector. In 2001, 60,500 tourists went whale watching from 10 locations around Iceland. In 2002, that number had grown to around 65,000 tourists. By 2010, numbers are predicted to exceed 100,000. The boom in whale watching generated around $8 million for the Icelandic economy in 2002.

Iceland: whaling or whale-watching?

Although whaling has been banned in Iceland since 1985, the whaling lobby is powerful. In March 2003, the Icelandic Government announced plans to take 100 minkes, 100 fin whales, and 50 endangered sei whales a year for the next two years. They claim they want to catch them for research, which is allowed by the International Whaling Commission.

But whale-watching companies and the tourism industry as a whole believe that a resumption in whaling would be bad news for the burgeoning whale-watching industry. The Icelandic Tourist Industry Association, whose members represent about 80 per cent of Iceland's turnover from tourism, agrees that whaling is bad for business. It has issued a statement saying that: 'Whale watching has become one of the most popular tourist activities in Iceland, providing considerable income for the

economy, as well as creating a very positive image for Iceland.' It added that to resume whaling, while governments in countries from which many tourists come do not recognise Iceland's right to hunt whales, would cause great damage to the Icelandic tourism industry.

Whale watching: where and what to see in the Arctic

You can watch whales in many parts of the world. The Arctic is one of the best.

- Norway's whale-watching season runs from May to January. You can see sperm whale, minke whale, fin whale, killer whale, pilot whale, and occasionally humpback whale.
- Iceland's season runs from May to September and you can see minke whale, humpback whale, fin whale, blue whale, killer whale, Atlantic white-sided dolphin, Atlantic white-beaked dolphin, harbour porpoise, and occasionally sei whale, sperm whale, pilot whale.
- In Greenland, the season runs from July to September and you can see fin whale, killer whale, minke whale, humpback whale, beluga, narwhal and harbour porpoise.
- Canada's whale-watching season runs from June to August. You can see bowhead, narwhal, beluga, fin whale, minke whale, killer whale, grey whale, humpback whale, pilot whale, Dall's porpoise, Northern Right Pacific white-sided dolphin, Atlantic white-sided dolphin, white-beaked dolphin, harbour porpoise and occasionally blue whale.
- In Alaska, the season runs from June to August and you can see fin whale, humpback whale, killer whale, grey whale and minke whale.

The work of WWF

WWF encourages carefully controlled whale watching because we believe it can promote whale, dolphin and porpoise conservation. For example, in the Andenes and Tysfjord areas of northern Norway, where sperm whales and orcas are commonly seen, WWF has helped develop whale watching. And in Iceland, WWF contributes to the funding for the Whale Centre, an interactive museum devoted to whales and the history of whaling in Husavik.

WWF provides educational material on whale conservation and the ecology of whales. WWF has also set up an English website – http://ngo.grida.no/wwfap/whalewatching – which gives information on whale watching in the Arctic.

The future?

Whale watching represents a significant source of revenue for many countries. It is a sustainable way of benefiting from whales which also contributes to public understanding of and support for marine conservation.

While hunting and watching wildlife can co-exist in some parts of the world, there is evidence to show that whaling causes hunted species to avoid boats and human beings. Iceland's whale-watching operators and the country's tourism industry believe a resumption in any sort of whaling will be detrimental to the country's fastest-growing business.

- The above information is from WWF-International.

© WWF-International

Oceans in crisis

Information from Greenpeace

Although oceans cover more than two-thirds of the planet's surface, it is clear that our oceans are limitless no more. For too long access to marine life has been largely open for use by anyone possessing the means to exploit it.

Rapid advances in technology have meant that the ability, reach and power of vessels and equipment used to exploit marine life now far outweigh nature's ability to maintain it. If left unchecked, this will have tragic consequences.

Whales, dolphins, porpoises and other cetaceans face many threats from human activities. Climate change, ozone depletion, toxic pollution, noise pollution and overfishing have left the oceans in a crisis which threatens the future of whales and the entire marine ecosystem.

Overfishing is the biggest single threat to marine ecology today.

Fishing fleets are now exceeding the oceans' limits. Some species have already been fished to commercial extinction.

The damaging impacts of overfishing do not stop at the 'targeted' fish species, or at those species caught 'incidentally' in fishing gear such as marine mammals or seabirds. Overfishing is increasingly affecting the marine ecosystems in which species are embedded. Scientists are warning that this will result in profound changes in our oceans, perhaps changing them for ever.

Modern fishing is dominated by industrialised vessels that use state-of-the-art fish-finding sonar devices to pinpoint schools of fish quickly and accurately. The ships also have fish-processing and packing plants, huge freezing systems, fishmeal processing plants, and powerful engines to drag enormous fishing gear through the ocean. Put simply: the fish don't stand a chance.

Almost everywhere, regulation of fishing vessels is woefully inadequate.

Greenpeace is campaigning to protect the oceans. We aim to limit or reverse the threats already imposed by humankind – including toxic pollution, noise pollution and overfishing – and ensure a safe future for marine ecosystems.

- The above information is from Greenpeace's web site which can be found at www.greenpeace.org.uk

© Greenpeace

Shark numbers 'at point of no return'

By Roger Highfield

The ocean's most fearsome predator has become common prey: shark populations have fallen to less than a quarter of their former size in the north-west Atlantic with the hammerhead particularly badly hit.

Some species are approaching the point of no return, and the team that reports the gloomy statistics today warns that current plans for marine reserves will not be enough to stop the decline caused by overfishing.

Existing protections for other large marine predators, such as sea turtles and tuna, should be extended to sharks, it says. Sharks are vulnerable to overfishing because they take many years to mature and have relatively few young per breeding cycle.

But they have been increasingly exploited in recent years, both as a 'by-catch' and as targets in their own right, either for food such as shark fin soup, or as ingredients in health and beauty products.

Until today's study, published in *Science*, the status of most shark species has been uncertain. Julia Baum and colleagues at Dalhousie University, Canada, analysed fishery records from the north-west Atlantic, one of the few datasets of its kind.

The researchers estimate that, with the exception of makos, all the species they studied have declined by more than half in the past eight to 15 years. The most striking example was hammerhead sharks, down by 89 per cent since 1986.

'The hammerheads concentrate in exactly the same places where the fleets fish for tuna and swordfish so they are hit because they are at the wrong place at the wrong time,' said Prof. Ransom Myers, a professor of biology at Dalhousie and co-author of the report.

The sharks routinely feed on the herring and squid commonly used for bait by the long-line fishermen, he said, making catching sharks a routine part of fishing for the other species.

Thresher sharks have declined by 80 per cent. Great white sharks, the predator in the film *Jaws*, have dropped by 79 per cent. The study found that in at least two fishing areas, no great white has been recorded since the early 1990s.

Tiger sharks have declined by 65 per cent and blue sharks by 60 per cent.

The team cannot conclude that the pattern of decline is consistent for the entire north Atlantic, but points out that it is likely as fishing levels are as intense elsewhere.

> *. . . they have been increasingly exploited in recent years . . . either for food such as shark fin soup, or as ingredients in health and beauty products*

'This is a worldwide phenomenon,' said Prof. Myers. 'There are only a few areas in the world where we have good data, but wherever we do, they show the same thing – the shark is in serious decline.'

Sharks could be protected by changing commercial fishing patterns. Some of the sharks migrate along set paths at specific times of the year. Prohibiting fishing during those periods could reduce the by-catch of sharks, said Prof. Myers.

Also, establishing refuges where all fishing was forbidden would give sharks, along with other fish, a safe haven where they could feed and reproduce safely.

The United States has forbidden harvesting of shark fins for shark fin soup, a favourite in Asia, but long-line fleets from Spain and Japan continue to harvest, said Prof. Myers.

Prof. David Conover, of the State University of New York, Stony Brook, said sharks are at the top of the food chain in the ocean and if they were to be wiped out by overfishing it could disrupt ecosystems.

'We know from many examples that once you start eliminating the predators at the top it has a ripple effect throughout the food web,' said Prof. Conover.

Trade in endangered species

Information from the Young People's Trust for the Environment

Man has always used wild animals and plants for their products, such as fruits and seeds for food, skins for clothing, wood for fires etc. Apart from its use for basic needs, wildlife has also been exploited for luxury items e.g. ornaments and fashion. At one time, when there were far fewer people on Earth and a lot more wildlife, such exploitation did not have any significant effect on the overall numbers of animals and plants. With over six billion people in the world today the situation is now very different. As a result of pressure from an ever-increasing human population, many species of animals and plants have been greatly reduced in numbers and they will not survive for much longer if we continue to kill them for luxury items. Modern technology and knowledge means that we can manufacture or find substitutes for products from endangered species: plastic for tortoise-shell or ivory, jojoba oil for whale oil, synthetic drugs for rhino horns and tiger bones. We can live very happily without leopard-skin coats, mahogany furniture, turtle soup or pet orang-utans.

Wildlife and the law

Over the last 30 years or so there has been a growing world-wide concern that trade in endangered species should be controlled. In 1973, representatives from 80 countries met in Washington to draw up a formula for trade controls and licences. As a result of this meeting the Convention on International Trade in Endangered Species (CITES) was formed. The purpose of CITES is to decide which species in trade are in danger of becoming extinct and to establish laws to stop them from being pushed any closer by international trade. There are now at least 126 member countries and their representatives meet every two years for discussions and to decide whether any changes are needed. Environmental organisations can attend the conferences to contribute to the debates and to lobby the delegates.

When a country joins CITES, its government must pass laws to control or prohibit trade in live or dead specimens and parts or derivatives of them. The amount of trade allowed depends on which 'Appendix' (group) the species has been listed in. The rules for deciding which species should be listed in which appendix were set down at the very first CITES conference in Berne, Switzerland, in 1976, although they have been revised since then. Any member country can put forward a species for listing, or changing to another appendix, but to be adopted, two-thirds of the delegates must vote for the proposal. A proposal is usually a scientific report summarising the best available information on the status of the species and the impact of trade on it. The Convention cannot control trade between two countries who are not CITES members, but fortunately the number of member countries is slowly increasing year by year. There are three appendices:

Appendix I

trade is totally banned for primarily commercial purposes.

MAHOGANY TABLES

CROCODILE SKIN HANDBAGS

CORAL CARVINGS

IVORY ORNAMENTS

Appendix II
potentially threatened species for which trade is allowed if there is 'no detriment' to the species: quotas (the numbers of individuals traded) may be imposed.

Appendix III
species requiring additional protection in their country of origin.

Enforcing the law
this is a difficult problem, especially when officials responsible for the enforcement don't take it seriously – and this happens all too often. Even CITES does not have a Law Enforcement Working Group. It is expensive to enforce a law and yet a law is useless unless it can be enforced.

Smuggling, i.e. illegal trading, is not easy to control. It is easier to stop the poverty-stricken poacher than the rich, influential businessman, or, worse still, corrupted government official. It is also difficult for the customs officer to identify the protected species in a big shipment of animals and plants – especially as they are often hidden or disguised.

Of all the hundreds of species of animals and plants involved in international trading laws, amongst some of the best-known examples are: big cats, whales, elephants, rhinos, bears, parrots, apes and rainforest plants. Here are two brief case histories:

Tigers

Fifty years ago there were eight subspecies of tiger, but three are now extinct. Today, all five remaining subspecies are endangered. The total number left in the world could be as low as 5,000. All tigers are in demand by Eastern countries because of their belief that tiger bones, claws, teeth and most other body parts have medicinal properties. China, South Korea and Taiwan are the main consumers but tiger products are also exported to Chinese communities in the rest of the world. China's own tigers are almost extinct so traders have turned to tigers in other countries and much illegal smuggling goes on. Tiger numbers are also declining because of the loss of their forest habitat and a shortage of prey.

Trade laws
Most tiger countries have laws protecting them, but they are often poorly enforced. Tigers are on Appendix I of CITES but five of the fourteen countries (which include China, India, Thailand, South Korea, Vietnam, Russia and Japan) have yet to join CITES – Bhutan, Burma (Myanmar), Cambodia, Laos and North Korea. However, these five, together with the CITES members, have voluntarily pledged to stop international trade in tiger products and, within their countries, to ban the use of tiger bone in traditional medicine. These countries have formed the Global Tiger Forum to discuss ways of working together to help tiger populations recover.

The future
The protection laws must be enforced somehow if the tiger is to survive. The US government's action of imposing trade sanctions on Taiwan, and threatening to do the same to China, may help. Hopefully, the Global Tiger Forum's discussions will bring about effective enforcement. Conservation organisations have set up projects to try and control poaching and to win the support of people who live in tiger areas, and to persuade people to use alternatives to traditional tiger-based medicines.

Fifty years ago there were eight subspecies of tiger, but three are now extinct

---

Plants

Although they are extremely important, and often beautiful, living organisms, plants are often overlooked when considering endangered species – animals usually attract more media attention. However, many thousands of species of plants need our help to prevent them from becoming extinct. Many commercial plants are grown in plantations or nurseries, but a large amount are still taken from the wild. Examples are the tropical hardwood trees, orchids, snowdrop bulbs, cacti and carnivorous plants, such as Venus flytraps. All these plants are removed from the wild either by the timber trade or for use as house and garden plants.

Trade laws
There are about 200 plant species listed on Appendix I by CITES. There are thousands more, including all orchids and cacti, on Appendix II. However, enforcement of the law is poor in most countries and many customs officers are not able to identify species in a shipment. To date, CITES has managed to list the Caribbean and Central American mahoganies on Appendix II, but fierce opposition by Brazil, Peru and Bolivia has prevented the Brazilian mahogany from also being listed – these countries have 90 per cent of these remaining mahogany trees. Japan is the biggest consumer of timber and living plants are sold mainly in North America, Europe and Japan.

The future
Various conservation organisations are either investigating the trade in plants or funding field projects. The charity 'Plantlife' has been set up specifically to save plants.

We can all help by refusing to buy items made from mahogany, or plants taken from the wild – check their source before buying.

■ The above information is from the Young People's Trust for the Environment's web site which can be found at www.yptenc.org.uk Alternatively, see page 41 for their address details.

© Young People's Trust for the Environment

Bushmeat

Information from the International Primate Protection League

What is bushmeat?

The term 'bushmeat' essentially refers to what we call 'game', meaning animals caught from the wild. Any animal, be it a deer, bird, monkey, even an elephant, can be bushmeat. Wildlife is hunted and eaten throughout the tropics, though the name 'bushmeat' is typically associated with West and Central Africa.

Why is bushmeat a problem?

Being hunted for meat is now thought to be the greatest threat to many species because the illegal, commercial bushmeat trade is decimating whole populations.

People think that eating monkey meat must somehow be related to poverty. It isn't that simple. Subsistence hunters, who move through the forest only killing enough food to feed themselves and their families, hardly affect animal numbers, but their way of life is a thing of the past.

These days bushmeat is big business. The modern-day bushmeat trade caters for wealthy people living in cities. Bushmeat is considered a delicacy and fetches correspondingly high prices. Many rural people will not eat it; either because they cannot afford it, or because they would rather sell it to earn money. Per kilo, bushmeat is more expensive than beef, pork or chicken.

How does the trade work?

Hunters move into the forests with the sole intention of killing as many animals as they can. They set snares, use guns, and hunt the larger monkeys and apes with dogs. Whole families can be wiped out. Pregnant or nursing females are the preferred target because they are slower moving and, if the hunter kills a mother with a baby, he gets two animals. But by removing the females, the hunters are rapidly driving the animals towards extinction.

All the hunting methods are completely unselective. The hunters do not worry, or may not even know, which species are endangered or protected under law. Everything is killed: from rats to gorillas.

The meat is carried out of the forest by hand, then taken away for sale by road or rail. This is where the logging industry causes problems. Timber extraction opens up large parts of the forest which gives hunters greater access to it, and logging trucks have been found carrying bushmeat. Workers living in large camps also create a ready market for the meat, and some companies have even employed hunters to feed their staff. Deforestation and bushmeat are therefore intimately linked.

The modern-day bushmeat trade caters for wealthy people living in cities. Bushmeat is considered a delicacy and fetches correspondingly high prices

---

Equally worrying is the discovery of bushmeat on sale in Paris, Brussels and London. In the UK, bushmeat has been seized at Heathrow, and confiscated from a London market. A West African restaurant, which has now closed, also offered bushmeat on its menu. The species being openly traded are often only rodents. However, even their importation contravenes health and safety laws, and shows how a channel for the smuggling of endangered species exists; a point proven by the discovery of monkey meat on sale in London.

What is the answer?

The solutions should be simple. Give the hunters other ways to earn a living, and, where appropriate, introduce alternative sources of protein into the local diet. The townsfolk must also be informed about the problem. No one wants to drive their country's wildlife to extinction, but until enough people realise how serious the problem is and how few animals are left, nothing will change. Wildlife protection laws must be enforced and conservationists must work with community groups to ensure social and cultural taboos concerning wildlife are respected.

What IPPL is doing

The sanctuaries that IPPL supports are on the frontline in the battle to halt the bushmeat trade. Their efforts for education, law enforcement, habitat protection and *in situ* captive breeding are exactly what are needed; though they are only part of the solution.

Bushmeat is a global problem that demands international co-operation. We are working with the Ape Alliance to encourage the UK and European governments to play a more active role in stopping the unsustainable trade.

Our UK Representative is also acting as an expert witness in the forthcoming prosecution of a London bushmeat trader.

■ The above information is from the International Primate Protection League's web site which can be found at www.ippl-uk.org

© International Primate Protection League IPPL (UK)

Endangered species

The threat from international trade

The British Government is a signatory to the Convention on International Trade in Endangered Species (CITES) which bans the trade in species of birds, animals and plants whose wild populations are threatened. The international trade hastens the extinction of these species in the wild and, in some cases, is the principal threat to their survival.

Some of the world's best-known animals are among the most endangered. For example:

- Elephants: Elephants are killed for their tusks by poachers who sell the ivory for use in the manufacture of items of jewellery and other trinkets for sale.
- Tigers: Tigers are killed for their bones which are used in traditional medicines in far-eastern communities where they are believed to have healing powers.
- Bears: In some Asian communities a bear's gall bladder is a highly prized remedy reputedly curing a wide range of ailments from haemorrhoids to liver disease. When traded on the black market, one gram of bear gall bladder has a value similar to that of one gram of cocaine or heroin.
- Rhinoceros: Rhinos have been hunted to the point of extinction by poachers who sell the horn on the black market to those who believe it to act as an aphrodisiac.

The very rarity of these and other endangered species inflates their value and means that large sums of money can be made by successful poachers and black marketeers.

We know that some endangered species, their parts and by-products are smuggled into Britain and in the London area Metropolitan Police Wildlife Officers have found ivory, reptile skins and even an endangered species of tropical fish being offered for sale. In 1993 a Wandsworth shopkeeper was cautioned for attempting to sell numerous items of

ivory and bags made from the skins of the African dwarf crocodile and the Nile monitor lizard, both of which are internationally recognised as in danger of extinction.

In February 1995, the Metropolitan Police seized several hundred medicinal products from Chinese pharmacies in central London. In the first police operation of its kind in Britain, 'Operation Charm' recovered medicines claimed to be made from tiger, rhinoceros and other endangered species.

The next time you hear of the tiger, elephant or rhinoceros being threatened with extinction, remember that this is not just a problem for other countries. There are people here in London who are directly threatening the survival of these and others of the world's rarest animals.

How you can help to protect endangered species

Many items made from endangered species are sold to tourists as holiday souvenirs. By buying these items you may be threatening the survival of the local wildlife. You may also risk having your goods seized by HM Customs and Excise when you return home.

It is sometimes difficult to tell which wildlife products are illegal to take home. Elephant ivory, spotted cat furs and sea turtle products are among the more obvious illegal items.

Be very careful when buying items made from reptile skins or coral as the trade in many of these species is also prohibited or may require special permits. It is also best not to buy live plants, birds or animals.

- Remember, if you are in any doubt, DON'T BUY!
- If you see any of these items being offered for sale in Britain, tell the police.
- If you have any information on wildlife crime please contact your local police.
- If you know of anybody who is committing crimes against wildlife, please phone Crimestoppers on 0800 555 111. Your call is free. You don't have to give your name, and your call could earn you a cash reward.

■ The above information is from the Metropolitan Police Service's web site which can be found at www.met.police.uk

Advice for travellers

Calling all travellers!

Think before you buy

You may be tempted to buy exotic souvenirs such as reptile skin handbags and ivory carvings on holiday, but you should remember that trade in many animals, plants and products made from them, is controlled internationally to safeguard endangered species. The trade in tourist souvenirs can threaten the most endangered species and you may also be breaking the law. If you are thinking of bringing back exotic souvenirs from abroad, you should check with Defra which items you can bring back before you leave as you may need a CITES permit. CITES goods imported without valid permits may be seized by Customs on your return and you could face an unlimited fine and/or imprisonment.

Over 800 species of animals and plants are currently banned from international trade and a further 30,000 strictly controlled by CITES and EU legislation including many corals, reptiles, orchids and cacti as well as tigers, rhinos, elephants and turtles. It is not easy to know which souvenirs or gifts to avoid buying and Defra's 'Souvenir Alert' campaign – in co-operation with the World Wildlife Fund (WWF-UK) – aims to raise awareness of the CITES controls amongst travellers. A brief guide to some of the products you are most likely to come across is provided here. International trade in some is banned altogether. Permits are required for others.

Remember, trade controls exist to protect these animals and plants. Your shopping decisions can help them survive.

Prohibited

Tigers, leopards and jaguars

CITES forbids trade in skins and products from many cat species such as the tiger, leopard and jaguar. Don't buy skins, handbags or coats made from them.

Traditional medicines

The tiger – one of the world's most

endangered species – is also threatened by demand for traditional medicines. Other medicines may contain tiger bone, rhino horn or other endangered plants and animals. If they do – and it is not always easy to tell – they cannot be imported or sold within the UK.

Turtles and tortoiseshell

Jewellery, combs, sunglasses or even whole shells from sea turtles are often available on exotic islands. If you want to help these species survive, please don't buy.

Elephant ivory

In 1997 CITES agreed to allow very limited export of ivory and elephant products. As far as tourist souvenirs are concerned this will only involve Zimbabwe and there will still be controls.

If you are visiting Zimbabwe, you are strongly advised to check with the Department for Environment, Food and Rural Affairs (Defra) before bringing anything back.

In all other African and Asian countries, export of these products is still banned even though you may see them for sale in shops, hotels, markets and even airport duty-free areas.

Remember these are only some of the products you may come across abroad – many more species are also banned from international trade.

Bushmeat

The meat of any wild animal hunted for food. Bushmeat may pose a health hazard to both humans and domestic livestock and its import into the UK from countries outside the EU is prohibited.

Permit required

It is best not to purchase live animals or birds on trips abroad. In any event, protected live animals and plants require an import permit, issued by Defra once they are satisfied that you also have an export permit from the country in which you obtained the goods. You must have both documents before animals and plants can be brought back into the EU.

Wildlife souvenirs

The top 10 illegal wildlife souvenirs based on seizures made by HM Customs and Excise at UK airports and ports are as follows

1	Traditional Chinese Medicine (including tiger, leopard, bear and musk deer)
2	Live reptiles (including snakes, lizards, chameleons, iguanas, tortoises & terrapins)
3	Coral
4	Alligator/Crocodile products
5	Snake and lizard products
6	Elephant ivory and skin products*
7	Plants (including American ginseng orchids and cycads)
8	Live birds (including parrots, macaws, owls, eagles and kites)
9	Queen conch shells
10	Caviar

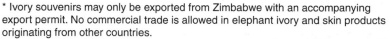

* Ivory souvenirs may only be exported from Zimbabwe with an accompanying export permit. No commercial trade is allowed in elephant ivory and skin products originating from other countries.

Source: HM Customs and Excise

Trade in dead specimens of plants and animals, and any parts derived from listed species, are also controlled so that trade does not threaten the survival of the species in the wild. You may bring back souvenirs made from certain CITES species where international trade is allowed, provided they are for your personal use and you have a CITES permit from the country of export.

Not all of the species involved are immediately obvious. You need to be clear what the legal requirements are for the products you want to buy. If you are not sure what a CITES export permit looks like, or where to apply for one, contact Defra before leaving. If you are still not sure, it may be best not to buy.

Orchids and cacti
Wild specimens of certain plants are banned from trade. Artificially propagated plants may be allowed into the country, subject to permit and phytosanitary regulations. Check with Defra first.

Coral
You need to be sure that coral necklaces, earrings and ornaments are not derived from endangered species. These are not always easy to identify on market stalls or in shops so if you're unsure, don't bring them home.

Further information on corals and particularly the identification of commonly traded CITES-listed corals can be found at www.arkive.org/coral

Reptile skins
Many reptile skins such as crocodiles, snakes and lizards are covered by strict European Union import controls. These products include snake-skin boots, bags, belts, shoes or watch straps. These controls vary depending on the species involved and the country of export – some only require export permits if the products being brought back are for personal use. Others are banned altogether – check which rules apply before you leave the UK.

Caviar
All species of sturgeon and their caviar are covered by controls. You may however bring up to 250 grams of caviar into the EU, for personal consumption. Check with Defra if you are in any doubt.

Channel Islands/Isle of Man
The Channel Islands and the Isle of Man are not part of the European Union. This means that permits are required for trade in CITES-listed species between the Islands and all countries that are Party to CITES – including the UK.

Remember
If you are interested in buying exotic souvenirs abroad, check it out with the Department for Environment, Food and Rural Affairs (Defra) before you leave the UK as you may need an export permit. Telephone: 0117 372 8691/8168. Fax: 0117 372 8206 E-mail: wildlife.licensing@defra.gsi.gov.uk or write to us at: Global Wildlife Division, Department for Environment, Food & Rural Affairs, 1/17 Temple Quay House, 2 The Square, Temple Quay, Bristol, BS1 6EB.

■ The above information is from the Convention on International Trade in Endangered Species' (CITES) web site which can be found at www.ukcites.gov.uk

© *Convention on International Trade in Endangered Species (CITES)*

The exotic pet trade and conservation

Information from IFAW

By Sheryl Fink and Bonnie Beresford

The worldwide buying and selling of wild animals as pets also affects the wild populations of these animals. The removal of animals from the wild for trade, either dead or alive, is one reason that many species become endangered.

The global wildlife trade is big business, estimated to be worth 25 billion dollars each year. Dead animals and their parts are used for everything from food and medicine to clothing and trinkets. Live animals are taken from the wild to be displayed in zoos and aquariums, for scientific research, and to be sold as exotic pets. The trade in wild animals as pets – known as the exotic pet trade – is just one part of the huge global trade in wildlife, but it can have a significant impact on wild animal populations.

Collecting for the pet trade
The majority of amphibians and reptiles in the pet trade are collected directly from the wild. The exotic pet industry creates a demand for these wild animals by making them popular and desirable as pets. The high death rates of pet amphibians and reptiles within the first year, combined with their low replacement cost, creates a never-ending market for these animals which results in even more individuals being removed from the wild. This creates a vicious cycle of catching, shipping, selling, buying, and dying. Certain methods used to collect wild herps, such as draining bogs and tearing dens apart, also destroy the animal's habitat.

Overcollecting

Overcollecting occurs when more animals are removed from the wild than are born and survive in the wild. Obviously, overcollecting will reduce the number of animals in a population. When overcollecting is combined with other threats, such as pollution, habitat loss, and disease, the results can be devastating to wild animal populations.

Captive breeding

If collecting wild animals for the pet trade threatens wild populations or destroys their habitats, one solution might be to breed and raise these animals in captivity. Many of the species found in the pet trade today are captivebred. Captive bred usually means that the animal was conceived and born in captivity, often from captive-bred parents. Some captive breeding operations are like farms, where snakes or lizards are raised instead of cows or pigs. However, even captive-breeding operations must occasionally refresh their stock from time to time with wild caught animals. But beware: the term 'captive bred' is also used by different people to mean different things. In some cases, females may be taken from the wild, their eggs hatched in captivity, and the offspring are then sold as 'captive bred'.

International Trade and CITES

The impact of global trade on certain species became such a concern that, in 1973, the Convention on International Trade in Endangered Species of Wild Fauna and Flora was created. This convention, more commonly referred to as CITES (pronounced 'sigh-teez'), is an international agreement that attempts to ensure that international trade does not threaten the survival of any wild animals or plants. There are currently over 30,000 different species – including those sold as exotic pets – that are now protected to varying degrees by the convention.

The illegal wildlife trade

Many countries that have joined CITES, such as the United States, have passed tough laws and created special wildlife police to help with

enforcement. However, there still exists a large, highly organised, and profitable illegal wildlife trade. The illegal wildlife trade is almost as profitable as the illegal drug trade, and the risks and penalties for smugglers are much lower. Smuggling of exotic animals takes many forms: endangered or illegally captured animals may be brought across borders hidden in concealed spaces, or they may be deliberately mis-identified as a common species or captive-bred individual.

The illegal wildlife trade is almost as profitable as the illegal drug trade, and the risks and penalties for smugglers are much lower

---

The elaborate illegal pet trade is fuelled by the legal pet trade which creates the demand for exotic animals and provides an incentive for poachers and smugglers. The illegal trade in endangered animals continues because illegal, wild-caught animals are cheaper than legal, captive-bred ones.

United States plays a major role in the wildlife trade, and is the world's largest consumer of live reptiles for the pet industry. In 2000 alone, at least 5.5 million live reptiles and amphibians were imported, with a reported value of 7.5 million dollars.

Certain types of animals are more vulnerable to overcollecting than others:

- Many reptiles, such as turtles and tortoises, are long-lived and take many years to reach the age when they can start producing babies. When these animals do reach reproductive age, they often give birth to only a few young, and only a few of these survive.
- Some reptiles, such as iguanas and turtles, are not only wanted as pets, but are also captured for their meat and skins.
- Some snakes spend the winter hibernating in large groups in dens. Collectors can then simply dig up the den to find thousands of sleepy, slow-moving, easily caught animals. As a result, the entire population in a region may be wiped out in a matter of hours. Animals with any of these characteristics cannot support large-scale collecting over the long term.

The International Fund for Animal Welfare works to improve the welfare of wild and domestic animals throughout the world by reducing commercial exploitation of animals, protecting wildlife habitats, and assisting animals in distress.

Traditional medicine

A major threat that few suspect

Traditional medicine (TM) has a global impact on wildlife, people, and the environment we share. The World Health Organisation (WHO) estimates that more than 4.8 billion people – 80 per cent of the world's population – use traditional medicines as their primary form of health care.

The widespread and growing popularity of TM threatens the survival of tigers, rhinoceros, bears, seahorses and other endangered species historically used in these traditional formulations.

In 1999, the global market in traditional medicines was estimated to be a US$20 billion business. Europe spent approximately US$7 billion on herbal remedies in 1999; North America spent US$3.8 billion; and Asian nations spent US$5.1 billion.

Since then, the popularity of alternative medicine, as measured by the utilisation of natural products, has grown exponentially throughout the world.

In addition, dramatic growth in E-commerce has augmented the availability of traditional medicines by creating new and increasingly accessible avenues of availability.

The increased availability of TM products that contain endangered animal parts and herbs has a sizeable impact on wildlife populations.

Through IFAW's work on traditional medicine issues, we promote the health and well-being of all species, including humans.

Many of the animals IFAW works to protect suffer tremendously from the demand for their body parts for use in TM. Among these are bears, hunted in Canada, Russia and the USA, and farmed in China; and seals, hunted in Canada and South Africa. Other wild species – including tigers, rhinos and leopards – are hunted throughout their ranges.

The widespread and growing popularity of traditional medicine threatens the survival of tigers, rhinoceros, bears, seahorses and other endangered species

---

IFAW is increasingly concerned with the plight of wildlife whose numbers are dwindling and who suffer great cruelty as a result of the growing global expansion of TM.

Four ways to reduce exploitation

IFAW believes that the preservation – and the welfare – of wildlife utilised in TM can only be achieved by reducing the commercial exploitation of these species.

Our approach to this challenge includes:

- Collaborating with members of the TM community and industry;
- Informing consumers about the connections between TM and the depletion of species;
- Encouraging the development of non-endangered herbal alternatives to traditionally used wildlife;
- Caring for individual animals harmed in illegal trade.

■ The above information is from the International Fund for Animal Welfare's web site which can be found at www.ifaw.org

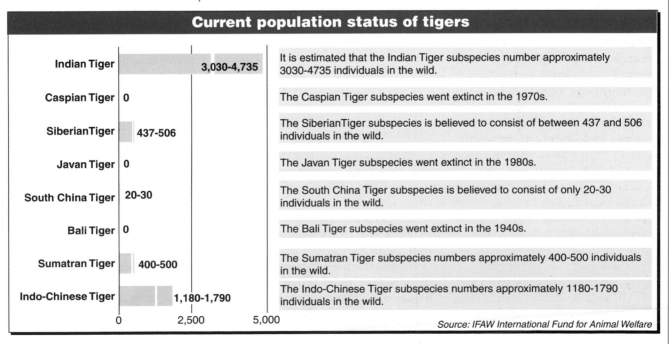

Current population status of tigers

Indian Tiger	3,030-4,735	It is estimated that the Indian Tiger subspecies number approximately 3030-4735 individuals in the wild.
Caspian Tiger	0	The Caspian Tiger subspecies went extinct in the 1970s.
Siberian Tiger	437-506	The Siberian Tiger subspecies is believed to consist of between 437 and 506 individuals in the wild.
Javan Tiger	0	The Javan Tiger subspecies went extinct in the 1980s.
South China Tiger	20-30	The South China Tiger subspecies is believed to consist of only 20-30 individuals in the wild.
Bali Tiger	0	The Bali Tiger subspecies went extinct in the 1940s.
Sumatran Tiger	400-500	The Sumatran Tiger subspecies numbers approximately 400-500 individuals in the wild.
Indo-Chinese Tiger	1,180-1,790	The Indo-Chinese Tiger subspecies numbers approximately 1180-1790 individuals in the wild.

Source: IFAW International Fund for Animal Welfare

Putting the con in conservation

After a history of keeping animals merely for human entertainment, zoos now have lofty aims of education and conservation. Most people's idea of zoo conservation is saving animals from extinction by breeding them in captivity and releasing them into the wild, and zoos would have us believe that they have plenty of success stories.

The number of vertebrate and invertebrate species classed as threatened (which includes endangered and vulnerable) in 2002 was 5,453. Even this may be an underestimate as other than mammals and birds only a small proportion of the total number of species has been assessed.[1]

So, if zoos are involved in 'conservation' one would expect to find a high number of these threatened species in their breeding programmes. Yet the most recent detailed study[2] found that 89% of the species kept in British zoos were not threatened species, and 25% of British zoos did not even keep any species classed as threatened.

Even many of the high-profile co-ordinated breeding programmes

amongst zoo bodies have no mechanism for returning animals to the wild, they simply provide for the continued breeding of certain species. When reintroduction programmes do take place they are often initiated by government wildlife agencies rather than by zoos.

Despite all the grandiose claims made in public, the zoo industry is more candid when discussing conservation amongst themselves. *International Zoo News* recently criticised two American zoos who had 'greeted the birth of Bactrian camels as a conservation success with these "endangered" animals', pointing out that 'all Bactrian camels in zoos – with the exception of a solitary male in Beijing – are of domestic origin, while only the wild form is endangered'.[3]

Lions are a popular 'exhibit' in zoos, but the vast majority of the lions 'are "generic" animals of hybrid or unknown sub-specific status, and therefore of little or no value in conservation terms'.[4]

What of zoo claims to have reintroduced endangered species to the wild?

The Arabian oryx is seen as the flagship of zoos' conservation image. Hunted to extinction in the mid-1970s, a captive-bred group was released in Oman in 1982 at a cost of $25 million.[5] 57 died of acute tuberculosis, partly due to the stress of being transported.[6] By 1999 only a quarter of the 400 animals had survived and 13 females were taken back into captivity 'for their own safety'.[7] Any success in reintroducing the oryx must be related to the co-operation of the local tribespeople who received payments for protecting them – perhaps if this was done originally they would never have become extinct.

The Hawaiian Crow ('alala) has been reduced to just one pair in the wild due to habitat destruction. Captive-reared birds started being released in 1993. 'By 1999, after 21

of the released captive-reared 'alalas had died, either from disease or through predation, the six remaining birds were returned to captivity. The release programme has been suspended indefinitely.'[8]

When Golden Lion tamarins were reintroduced to Brazil in the mid-80s, only 30 of the 100 released survived, having failed to adapt to life in the wild.[7]

In 1991 a lethal virus was identified in a captive-bred tamarin just three days before the monkey was due to be released into an area where the virus was unknown.[9] Reintroduction plans for the woolly monkey were also cancelled due to the discovery of a virus amongst the captive-bred population.[10] During the 1980s, Gopher tortoises were released in California with the resultant deaths of 40,000 wild desert tortoises due to the spread of a virus.[7]

According to one zoo director 'We can find evidence that only 16 (11%) of the 145 reintroduction projects contributed to the establishment of a self-sustaining wild population.'

Zoocheck Canada commented in response: 'Many of these examples are translocations into previously occupied or vacant habitat, and were not pivotal to the survival of the species.'[11]

Zoos still take animals from the wild. Wild-caught gorillas can still be found in British zoos and last year there was worldwide controversy when four wild-caught gorillas were traded between zoos in Africa and Asia. In the last 10 years 1,046 wild-caught elephants have been traded to zoos and circuses[12] and over 70% of elephants in European zoos today were wild-caught.[13]

In August the 11 elephants that campaigners fought hard to keep in the wild were sent to a life of captivity in America. The young elephants have already seen their families killed in a mass 'cull'. From the wilds of Swaziland to a shared enclosure of just five acres, these elephants will remain in zoos for the rest of their lives. Alternative homes in Africa for these elephants were turned down.

Japanese zoos have been criticised for planning to obtain five wild-caught endangered Sumatran elephants, as well as polar bears from Canada.

Aquariums are even bigger culprits at taking animals from the wild, particularly due to the short life span of many aquatic species in captivity and the increase in aquariums. It is generally recognised that for each animal caught in the wild who reaches captivity in another country, several others will have died during capture, confinement and transportation.

To really protect wild animals we need to protect their environment. Even if captive-breeding programmes were successful in producing a viable population capable of being returned to the wild, history shows that they will not survive if the fundamental reasons for their endangerment are not addressed.

If any captive-breeding programme were to be successful, it would have to be as close as possible to the ultimate release site, particularly in terms of climate, habitat and fauna. The animals need space appropriate to their needs and populations large enough to provide a suitable gene pool and a natural social balance of the species, with minimal human contact.

Not only does it make more sense in conservation terms to protect animals in their natural habitat, but it is also much cheaper. For the cost of keeping 16 black rhinos in captivity, the 492,000-hectare Garamba National Park in Zaire 'protects an entire ecosystem that is home to 31 northern white rhino, 4,000 elephant, 30,000 buffalo, the entire giraffe population of Zaire, 14 other ungulate species, 16 carnivore species, 10 primate species, and 98 small mammal species'.[14]

Zoos really have put the con in conservation.

Zoo director David Hancocks commented: 'There is a commonly held misconception that zoos are not only saving wild animals from extinction but also reintroducing them to their wild habitats. The confusion stems from many sources, all of them zoo-based . . . In reality, most zoos have had no contact of any kind with any reintroduction program.'[15]

Zoo-bred animals have a greater chance of ending up in circuses, private collections, vivisection labs, the meat trade, or being 'culled' in the zoo than they do of being returned to the wild.

'So far, zoos have had only a modest, and in some cases insignificant, involvement in re-introduction efforts, yet, as an industry, they have grossly overstated their own importance in this area, often for self-serving reasons' Zoocheck Canada.[16]

References

1 'Summary Statistics for Globally Threatened Species', IUCN: www.redlist.org/info/tables/table1.html

2 Official Zoo Health Check 2000, BFF 2001

3 International Zoo News, Vol 49, No 7 (2002) pp386-388

4 International Zoo News, Vol 49, No 5 (2002), pp258-259

5 BBC Wildlife, July 1998, pp65-69 and Sad Eyes and Empty Lives, CAPS factsheet

6 Who Cares for Planet Earth? Dr Bill Jordan, 2001, p74

7 Sad Eyes and Empty Lives, CAPS factsheet

8 BBC Wildlife, January 2003, pp62-63

9 Who Cares for Planet Earth? Dr Bill Jordan, 2001, p73

10 'Release', CAPS magazine, Summer 2002, pp6-7

11 Who Cares for Planet Earth? Dr Bill Jordan, 2001, p77

12 Wildlife Times, Winter 2002/2003

13 A Review of the Welfare of Zoo Elephants in Europe Clubb and Mason, RSPCA, 2002, p28

14 Who Cares for Planet Earth? Dr Bill Jordan, 2001, p79

15 Quoted in Who Cares for Planet Earth? Dr Bill Jordan, 2001, pp67-68

16 Who Cares for Planet Earth? Dr Bill Jordan, 2001, p66

■ The above information is from the Captive Animals' Protection Society. Visit their web site at www.captiveanimals.org

Red alert over rare species

By James Randerson

The well-known 'Red List' that details which species are threatened with extinction is inaccurate, according to a new assessment. It concludes the list fails to reflect the true threat to species, by not taking full account of the threat posed by people.

The Red List, which is compiled by the World Conservation Union (IUCN), gauges a species' risk of extinction mainly on the basis of its population size, rate of decline and geographic range.

But Alexander Harcourt and Sean Parks at the University of California, Davis, argue that this is not enough. They compare an endangered species to a house that has been left unlocked. The house is vulnerable to burglary, but it only becomes threatened when there is a burglar nearby.

In the same way, a small population of animals susceptible to extinction only becomes actively threatened when it is being poached or its habitat is destroyed. Harcourt and Parks advocate modifying the Red List criteria to include local human population density.

Although a large number of people nearby may not in itself be a threat, they argue that hunting, pollution and habitat destruction, for example, are all likely to increase as people encroach on wildlife. What is more, data on human density is readily available. 'We have the numbers, why not use them?' says Harcourt.

Low to high

To illustrate their point, the researchers reassessed 200 primate species from the 1996 Red List. They found that 17 species designated as being at relatively low risk by the Red List should now be reassigned as high priority. Two such species are Wied's tufted-ear marmoset (*Callithrix kuhlii*) and the golden lion tamarin (*Leontopithecus rosalia*) from South America.

Contrary to the expectations of many, the researchers also found that two high-profile species, the gorilla and the pygmy chimpanzee, or bonobo, should be downgraded to a lower level of threat.

A small population of animals susceptible to extinction only becomes actively threatened when it is being poached or its habitat is destroyed

But Craig Hilton-Taylor, Red List Programme Officer based in Cambridge, England, says that the IUCN has already introduced a specific classification system for threats such as human density. The system runs in parallel to the main Red List classification.

Besides, part of the Red List's value is that you can make comparisons with past assessments, he says, and tweaking the criteria would make this impossible. 'We've been asked by everyone, please don't change the system again,' says Hilton-Taylor.

Harcourt maintains that making explicit threats part of the criteria is not only more accurate, it may also help highlight future problems. Matt Walpole, a conservation researcher at the University of Kent at Canterbury, England, agrees: 'Where [population] data is lacking, it might be a useful way of flagging up potentially threatened species.'

■ The above information is from the *New Scientist*'s web site which can be found at www.newscientist.com

The 25 most endangered primates – 2002

1. Greater bamboo lemur	17. White-headed langur
2. Perrier's sifaka	18. Grey-shanked doue
3. Silky sifaka	19. Tonkin Snub-nosed monkey
4. Black-faced lion tamarin	20. Yunnan Snub-nosed monkey
5. Buff-headed capuchin	21. Guizhou Snub-nosed monkey
6. Northern muriqui	22. Eastern black crested gibbon
7. Miss Waldron's red colobus	23. Mountain gorilla
8. Roloway guernon	24. Cross River gorilla
9. White-naped mangabey	25. Sumatran orang-utan
10. Tana River mangabey	
11. Tana River red colobus	
12. Sanje mangabey	
13. Natuna banded leaf monkey	
14. Pig-tailed snub-nosed monkey	
15. Delacour's langur	
16. Golden-headed langur, Cat Ba langur	

Source: UNEP-WCMC

World must face up to loss of plant and animal species

Information from the Royal Society

Governments must adopt a global plan for assessing how quickly plant and animal species are becoming extinct, according to a report published by the Royal Society, the UK national academy of science, ahead of a meeting of the United Nations Convention on Biodiversity in London on 21-23 May 2003.

The Society has prepared a 'framework for measuring biodiversity' to help governments of the world to achieve the target of 'a significant reduction in the current rate of biodiversity loss by 2010', which was agreed at the World Summit on Sustainable Development in Johannesburg in September 2002.

Professor Peter Crane, Director of Kew Gardens and chair of the Royal Society working group on biodiversity, said: 'The living world is disappearing before our eyes. Around one in ten of all the world's bird species and a quarter of its mammals are officially listed as threatened with extinction, while up to two-thirds of other animal species are also endangered. These losses have accelerated over the last two hundred years as a direct and indirect consequence of the growth in human populations, wasteful use of natural resources and associated changes to the environment.'

He added: 'Although we have a feel for the scale of the loss, we often lack specific and accurate information about how badly individual species and their habitats are suffering. Without this information, it is very difficult to work out whether global efforts to save these species are being successful. And it is essential that they do succeed because many of the world's poorest people directly depend for their livelihoods on the diversity of plant and animal species and their habitats.'

The framework outlines the best approach to measuring the damage inflicted on wildlife and their habitats, using the most reliable scientific methods. It can be applied to long-term monitoring programmes as well as emergency situations, such as an oil tanker disaster.

Around one in ten of all the world's bird species and a quarter of its mammals are officially listed as threatened with extinction

---

The report recommends that the framework should be applied routinely by those commissioning,

funding and undertaking measurements of biological diversity. Scientists should focus urgently on making available to each other, and more generally, existing information on species and their habitats, for instance, by making better use of the world-wide web.

Prof. Crane said: 'Scientists will only be able to deliver the required information about the loss of species and their habitats if governments and their agencies change their reluctance to fund projects that would bring together data quickly from a wide range of sources. And only then will we be able to identify where the real gaps in our knowledge are.'

He added: 'If we are to achieve a significant reduction in the rate of species loss by 2010, current monitoring programmes will need to be expanded and new ones will need to be put into action. These will require a marked increase in funding and better co-ordination between NGOs, academic scientists, and governmental and inter-governmental agencies.'

The meeting of the UN Convention on Biological Diversity, which will include members of the Royal Society working group on biodiversity, is being held to:
- review means in place for achieving the target of significantly reducing the rate of biodiversity loss by 2010;
- review and agree on approaches for measuring and assessing achievements towards meeting the 2010 target; and
- review and agree on the most appropriate approaches for reporting on progress.

■ The above information is from the Royal Society's web site which can be found at www.royalsoc.ac.uk
© The Royal Society

British endangered species

Information from Care for the Wild International

What is an endangered species?

If a species is said to be endangered, then it is in danger of going extinct if the reasons that are causing its numbers to decline are not identified and the problems put right.

Vulnerable species are those who are declining in numbers quite rapidly.

Rare species are those which are only found in a particular area, or in a habitat that is found only in a few places in Britain.

The term 'threatened' is used to describe species that are included in all these categories. This term is frequently used when talking about British species.

Why do species become threatened?

Different species are suited to different habitats or types of vegetation, they live where they find the other species that they feed on and where they are able to build their homes, and where they are able to protect their young. The numbers of many animal and plant species in Britain have declined in recent years due to the loss of the habitat in which they are usually found. Different habitat types are lost when we build on them to accommodate an increasing human population or remove them to increase the efficiency of agriculture. Changes in the climate also affect some habitat types.

What can be done?

If we protect the habitats that threatened animal species are found in then they will also be protected. To do this, we need to identify the animals and plants that are declining by counting them, we need to see if they are found in all of the places that they used to be found, and we need to find out as much as is possible

about their lives and what they need to live.

We need to ensure that habitats that have decreased in recent years are prevented from declining any further. We can do this by ensuring that they are not built on, by replanting trees where they have been cut down, by not polluting our waterways and by creating new areas of rare habitats. There are laws that help us to do this and the Government draws up guidelines with help from nature organisations to ensure that threatened species are protected to prevent them becoming extinct.

Some of the threatened species in Britain

In Britain we have lost over 100 species this century. Species that have not been recorded in Britain in the last 10 years include fish called sturgeon and houting, several species of beetles, a moth and several species of moss and lichen.

Recently species and habitats that are most threatened in Britain have been prioritised and species action plans have been written for them. The factors that are causing them to decline and what can be done to help them are included in these action plans.

Here are some examples of the species that are most threatened in Britain.

Mammals

Water vole (*Arvicola terrestris*)
The water vole is a small mammal similar in appearance to a mouse, it is found mainly in lowland areas near water. A recent population estimate suggested that the total British population was 1,200,000.

The water vole was once common and widespread throughout Britain but its habitat has become fragmented and has declined because of disturbance along our rivers. Pollution of waterways and accidental poisoning is also linked to the decline of water vole, as is predation by mink.

Ways of helping the water vole population include making sure that their habitat is not disturbed in the future, avoiding the use of pesticides near areas known to have water voles and making sure that landowners know if they have them on their land and what they can do to help them.

*European otter (**Lutra lutra**)*
The European otter is a semi-aquatic mammal that feeds mainly on fish. The number of otters in the United Kingdom has declined a lot since the 1950s and the species was lost from many areas by 1980. They can now be found in Wales, SE England and much of Scotland. The otter is protected by several agreements between the UK and other countries that also have populations.

The numbers have declined because of pollution in waterways; this also reduces the amount of available food for them. Sites where the otters can breed and rest have declined, and they are also sometimes accidentally killed on the roads and in fish traps.

There have been lots of surveys of otters and some riverside areas have been especially designed for their needs. This is done by ensuring that they are surrounded by deciduous trees and shrubs and other types of habitat that otters require, it may also include creating log piles and artificial holts (breeding nests). Fortunately, now there is evidence that in certain parts of the UK the otter is extending its range and maybe increasing locally.

Bechstein's bat (Myotis bechsteinii)

There are 14 species of bat living in the British Isles, all of which are protected by law. Bat species are particularly threatened because they require safe places for them to hibernate and to sleep. Many species roost in old hollow trees, the number of these has declined a lot over recent years, increasingly forcing bats to roost in old buildings. Here they may be disturbed, their access holes may be blocked up accidentally and they are badly affected if woodwork in the building is treated with chemicals for woodworm.

Bats are difficult to study and they reproduce at a low rate. Bechstein's bat is one of the rarest species; it is a tree-dwelling species preferring broad-leaved woodland. There are only thought to be around 1,500 individuals left in the UK.

There are many specialist bat groups around Britain who are actively involved with bat conservation. Known hibernation sites have been protected against disturbance and bat boxes have been provided in areas where roost sites are limited.

Birds

Marsh warbler (Acrocephalus palustris)

The marsh warbler comes to Britain in the summer to breed. In 1980 there were thought to be 50-80 pairs. During the 1980s what was thought to be the main population, which was found in Worcestershire and the Severn and Avon valleys, declined rapidly and none were recorded there in 1989. A population was established in Kent in the 1970s which is thought to have over 25 pairs and there are now also several other pairs thought to breed in surrounding counties. There are also populations of this species in other European countries.

Changes in vegetation type are thought to be responsible for the decline of the Avon valley

population. Changes in the climate are thought to have affected the species as a whole. Also, the populations of this species have become quite fragmented – they are found only in a few areas – this makes it difficult for different birds to meet. Disturbance by bird watchers and people along rivers also affects how well the birds breed.

Action to help to conserve the marsh warbler is being carried out by wildlife trusts and conservation organisations in areas known to have populations at present, and in areas that used to have populations. They monitor the number of birds that are present, they work to increase the amount and types of habitat that the species needs and try to reduce disturbance of the nests.

Nightjar (Caprimulgus europaeus)

The nightjar is also a summer migrant, its numbers and places where it can be found have both declined during the last 100 years. In 1992 there were thought to be 3,400 males coming to Britain, they are mainly found in southern England but there are some populations as far north as Scotland. The species has also declined in Europe.

The most important British habitats for this species are lowland heathland and young forestry plantations. Heathland in the UK has declined as more land is used for farming and building development. Cultivated land is not suitable habitat

for the birds as it does not support many of the big insects that the nightjar likes to feed on. The nightjar nests in new plantations where there are still spaces of bare ground between the trees.

The nightjar has several laws that protect it and conservation initiatives work towards maintaining the different habitat types that they require.

Amphibians

Natterjack toad (Bufo calamita)

The natterjack toad is the rarest amphibian species native to Britain. It can be found at 4 natural sites in Scotland and 35 in England. In order to help its conservation it has also been introduced into 13 further sites.

Like other toads it lives most of its life on land, in holes beneath tree roots or in hedges, but returns to ponds to breed. It is found in heathland, sand dunes and saltmarsh habitats, but it has declined as the amount of these habitats has declined. It also suffers when the pools that it spawns in are polluted. Toads are also at risk from predation and being run over.

During the summer they shed their skins several times and they hibernate in October and November. When they emerge in March or April they make their way back to the pond where they were born. This makes it very important to conserve its habitat and to know exactly where any members of this species are present

Plants

Lady's slipper orchid (Cypripedium calceolus)

There are 54 species of orchid that grow in Britain. Many of these species are rare, but their seeds are so light that the wind can carry them hundreds of miles so they are often found in many different places in small numbers. Development of orchids is very slow; it can take years for them to grow large enough for them to flower. This characteristic makes orchids very vulnerable as any decline in numbers would take a long time to recover.

The lady's slipper orchid grows on limestone grassland that is only moderately grazed by sheep and cows. The species has suffered a severe decline and only naturally occurs at one site, although the colony is growing.

The species has declined due to people picking them and trampling on them, as well as their surrounding habitat being destroyed by too much grazing.

The species is protected by law and the site where it is found is subject to careful habitat management and wardening. There is also work going on to introduce the plant to other areas. These may be areas where it used to be found, if the habitat is still suitable, or new areas that have all of the characteristics it requires. It is hoped that by 2004 populations of the species will be found at 5 sites.

■ Care for the Wild International is an accomplished wild animal welfare and conservation charity. For more information please see their website at www.careforthewild.com or see their address details on page 41.

© Care for the Wild International

Endangered wildlife and habitats

In the last century, around 170 species of plants and animals became extinct in the UK, such as the mouse-eared bat, the Norfolk damselfly and the summer lady's tresses orchid. Many continue to decline at a rapid rate

Endangered wildlife

Between 10 and 20% of native species in Great Britain are considered 'threatened' and similar proportions of invertebrates and plants are 'nationally scarce'. Some species, however, will always be rare because their habitat is naturally very small or they are at the geographical limit of their natural range.

■ Threatened species are either endangered, vulnerable, or rare based on the International Union for the Conservation of Nature's (IUCN) criteria.

■ Nationally scarce species are those present in only 16 to 100 ten km^2 in Great Britain.

Similar information for mammals and birds at risk is not available for Great Britain since the IUCN threat status is assessed internationally.

Habitat loss

Examples of habitats that have experienced a significant loss in area include:

Lowland heath

There has been an 83% decrease in the area of lowland heath since the 1800s. In Dorset, heathland used to cover an area of 389km^2. By the late 19th century the expansion of Bournemouth and agricultural use of the heathland had reduced the area to 277km^2. Commercial afforestation in the early 20th century and further urban expansion in recent decades caused further loss and fragmentation. By the end of the 1990s it was estimated that no more than 58km^2 of heathland would remain.

Hedgerows

Between 1984 and 1990 hedgerows declined through removal or neglect, at an estimated rate of 22,000km per year. Since 1990, the rate of decline was lower, 18,000km per year. Much of this loss is due to larger agricultural fields. New hedgerows have been planted, but these have less wildlife associated with them than established hedgerows, which support over 600 plant, 1,500 insect, 65 bird and 20 mammal species.

Grassland

The vast majority of all managed grasslands are species-poor, improved grasslands. In agricultural areas these have replaced species-rich neutral, calcareous and acidic grasslands. Between 1930 and 1984, the area of unimproved neutral grasslands decreased by 97%. The remaining patches of these grasslands are now

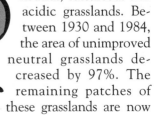

important reserves of increasingly rare species. Between 1978 and 1990 wild flowers once commonly found in meadows and chalk grasslands declined significantly. There have also been losses of high quality meadow habitats. Meadows are being created in an attempt to balance this loss, but they are of a lower quality than the mature meadows.

Main threats to habitats and wildlife

For many years there has been a growing concern over the impact of human activities, whether directly or indirectly, on species, habitats and natural ecosystems. Many of the landscapes that we now consider to be 'traditional' have been influenced or modified in some way by human activities. The past 100 years have seen a considerable increase in the pace and scale of human intervention in the natural environment, coupled with dramatic losses in biodiversity.

There are three main threats to habitats and wildlife.

- Direct loss of habitat and species from agricultural improvements, urban development, mineral extraction and afforestation.
- Fragmentation, or the splitting up of continuous blocks of habitat and species into disconnected pockets.
- Degradation, which occurs when a habitat is no longer managed in an appropriate manner, for example overgrazing on upland moors and undergrazing on lowland heaths.

Reversing the decline

To halt the rapid decline in habitat and species diversity, agreements at both the national and international level were established. These include the Bern, Bonn, Ramsar and CITES (Convention for the International Trade in Endangered Species) Conventions of the late 1970s and early 1980s.

For many years there has been a growing concern over the impact of human activities, whether directly or indirectly, on species, habitats and natural ecosystems

---

One of the most influential conventions attempting to address the threats facing habitats and species globally was the United Nations Conference on Environment and Development (the Earth Summit) at Rio de Janeiro in 1992. It recognised that biodiversity should be treated as a global resource to be protected according to the principles of ecological, economic and social sustainability. The summit also identified the need to establish a programme of sustainability at the local level: Agenda 21.

The UK signed the Convention on Biological Diversity (CBD), which led to the establishment of the UK Biodiversity Action Plan. This is the UK's initiative to maintain and enhance biodiversity. It recognises 391 species and 45 habitats as priorities for action.

The Agency has a duty under the Environment Act 1995 to have a regard for conservation with respect to its pollution control and waste management functions, and to further conservation with respect to all of its other functions. In order to achieve the objective of sustainable development, the Agency has been requested to pay particular attention to its conservation duties.

■ The above information is from the Environment Agency's web site which can be found at www.environment-agency.gov.uk

© *The Environment Agency 2003*

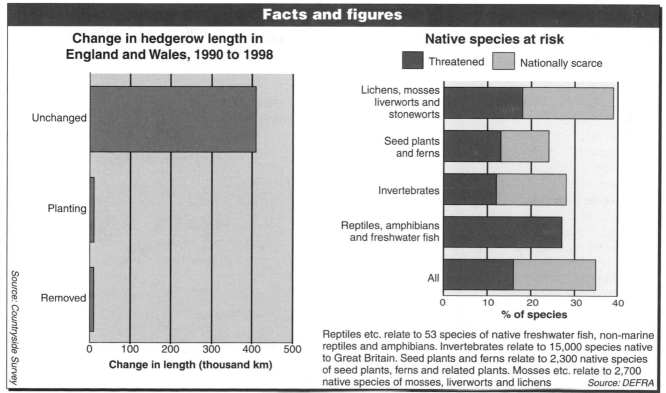

Facts and figures

Change in hedgerow length in England and Wales, 1990 to 1998

Source: Countryside Survey

Change in length (thousand km)

Native species at risk

Threatened / Nationally scarce

% of species

Reptiles etc. relate to 53 species of native freshwater fish, non-marine reptiles and amphibians. Invertebrates relate to 15,000 species native to Great Britain. Seed plants and ferns relate to 2,300 native species of seed plants, ferns and related plants. Mosses etc. relate to 2,700 native species of mosses, liverworts and lichens   Source: DEFRA

Mammals facts

Information from Mammals Trust UK

What is a mammal?

Mammals all share certain characteristics:

- They have hair that covers all or part of their body
- Are warm-blooded and can keep their body temperature more or less constant
- Give birth to live young
- Rear young on milk

They have been classified in nine groups (called orders). They are:

1. Artiodactyls (deer)
2. Carnivores (foxes, wildcats and mustelids)
3. Cetaceans (whales, dolphins and porpoises)
4. Chiroptera (bats)
5. Insectivores (hedgehogs, moles, and shrews)
6. Lagomorphs (rabbits and hares)
7. Marsupials (wallabies and kangaroos)
8. Pinnipeds (seals)
9. Rodents (mice, rats and voles)

Most at risk

Of the 66 mammal species that are ordinarily or seasonally found in the UK, several have experienced dramatic declines in recent years. The big ten that wildlife experts have highlighted as the most at risk are:

1. Water vole
2. Red squirrel
3. Wildcat
4. Pine marten
5. Greater horseshoe bat
6. Barbastelle bat
7. Bechstein's bat
8. Bottle-nosed dolphin
9. Harbour porpoise
10. Northern right whale

Mammals as quality of life indicators

A healthy environment is important to all mammals, including humans. Therefore, mammals serve as excellent indicators of the quality and health of our environment. If their world is disappearing or being degraded, it makes sense to investigate whether their loss has implications for us.

Currently, the British government uses birds to measure the overall status of our wildlife and environment. At MTUK, we believe that these assessments would be more relevant by using mammal information. However, at present we don't know enough about them to be able to make these assessments. MTUK is, therefore, committed to gathering as much information about them as possible.

Why are they in trouble?

Mammals are an important part of the amazing fabric of life on earth. They have survived for thousands of years and have helped shape our history and culture. Imagine *Wind in the Willows* without the water vole 'Ratty', or *Alice in Wonderland* without the sleepy dormouse.

Today, the kind of problems they face include:

- Disappearing habitats – As pressure for homes, roads and other development increases, mammals are deprived of their natural habitats. Remaining mammal populations are often left isolated, compromising future survival;
- Conflict with non-native species – Introduced alien species, such as grey squirrels, have a huge impact on our native mammals through predation, competition, hybridisation and transmission of disease;
- Toxic habitats – Industrialised pollutants and agri-chemicals can kill our mammals. In addition, non-lethal effects include reducing reproductive success, weakening immunity and also indirectly reducing food and/or habitat availability;
- Conflict with man – In the last few centuries, culling has been responsible for the decimation of at least 10 UK mammal species. Other man-related causes of death include hunting for sport or animal products and death on the roads.

■ The above information is from Mammals Trust UK's web site which can be found at www.mtuk.org

© *Mammals Trust UK*

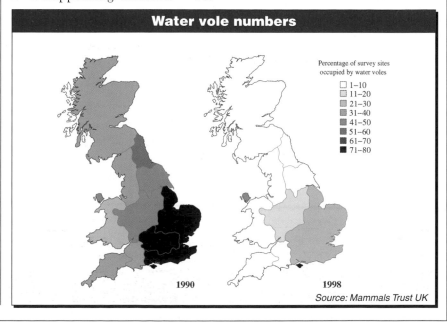

Water vole numbers

Percentage of survey sites occupied by water voles

- 1–10
- 11–20
- 21–30
- 31–40
- 41–50
- 51–60
- 61–70
- 71–80

1990

1998

Source: Mammals Trust UK

Otter numbers show five fold increase

By Charles Clover,
Environment Editor

England's otter population has risen fivefold since the low point of its decline in the late 1970s, said a report by the Environment Agency and the Wildlife Trusts in May 2003.

The otter is on course to return to every part of England where it was found more than 50 years ago – when it was evenly distributed throughout the country – but at present inhabits just over a third of sites surveyed.

The study, undertaken with help from the water companies and English Nature, found that of 3,327 sites surveyed between 2000 and 2002, 1,137 showed evidence of otters, either prints or droppings.

Otters were found in 35 per cent of all sites surveyed in 2000-02, a sizeable increase since the first survey of its kind was carried out between 1977 and 1979. This found otters in only 5.8 per cent of sites.

Conservationists say the otter is a predator at the top of the food chain, so its health is important not only in itself, but as a reflection of the health of rivers and wetlands generally.

In the 1950s and 1960s the otter suffered a serious decline throughout its European range. The main reason was thought to have been the introduction of aldrin and dieldrin, the persistent organochlorine pesticides, which built up in fatty tissue and affected reproduction.

The 1977 survey found that the only significant population of otters remaining in England was in the South West and along the Welsh border, with small and fragmented populations in East Anglia and northern England.

Two surveys since then have shown a gradual recovery, but this has been markedly slower than for other predators, such as the peregrine falcon and sparrowhawk, affected by organochlorine compounds. Conservationists say this may reflect otters' slower breeding rate.

Other factors included poor river quality and habitat loss, increased human disturbance, an apparent decline in fish productivity and increased danger on the roads from the growth in traffic.

Andrew Crawford of the Environment Agency, the survey's author, said the results showed the otter recovering, but some areas had recorded substantial growth while others had experienced little or none.

Evidence of otters has increased significantly on the Trent river system since the 1970s, but parts of the North West have recorded only a small rise in positive sightings. The South East has had only a low increase, possibly because of its small otter population and the disproportionately large numbers of deaths on roads and railway tracks.

Mr Crawford said: 'Otters are not increasing as fast as we would like in some areas and we will need to concentrate on ways to protect the otter from cars, which continue to be one of the biggest threats.'

Martin Spray, acting director general of the trusts, said: 'There are still some significant gaps in otter distribution throughout England. Only about one-third of the sites surveyed had evidence of otters and we are still some time away from full recovery of historical otter numbers.'

© *Telegraph Group Limited, London 2003*

> *The otter is on course to return to every part of England where it was found more than 50 years ago*

England's rainforest

A bleak corner of Essex is being hailed as England's rainforest. Endangered species under threat from development plan

By John Vidal

It is one of the more unlikely ecological finds in Britain in a generation. A derelict oil terminal beside a giant superstore in one of the unloveliest corners of Essex has been found to have more wildlife per square foot than any national nature reserve. It has been described as 'England's little rainforest' and is becoming a place of pilgrimage for scientists.

But before anyone has a chance to protect it, one of deputy prime minister John Prescott's new development quangos has bought it and received outline planning permission to destroy the most important bit as part of the Thames Gateway expansion of London.

For Matt Shardlow, who runs the invertebrate conservation trust Buglife, the former Occidental site on Canvey Island is an oasis in a landscape of oil refineries, new housing, massive roundabouts and drive-though McDonald's. Laid out with concrete roads and street lighting, it has been left untouched for more than 30 years.

To the untutored eye, it is a scrappy place, with burnt-out cars, pipes and plastic bags lying around. There are rusting shopping trolleys and old bikes in the ditches and the BP Coryton oil refinery looms beyond it.

Some patches of the 100 hectare (240 acre) site have been set on fire, others have been used as a motocross track. For planners, landscape designers and people who like their nature adorned with lawns, prim hedges and carefully planted beds, it is an unruly nightmare. 'This is nature down and dirty,' said Mr Shardlow.

A full audit of the site has not been completed, but in less than two years' study it has already been found to be home to at least 1,300 species, including 30 on the UK 'red list' of endangered species. Five of the UK's most threatened bumblebee species live here, including the rare Shrill carder bee. A ground beetle and a weevil not seen in 77 years and thought to be extinct have turned up and several insects so rare they have not been given English names have been discovered.

There are skylarks, badgers and at least 300 species of moth, including three species which Mr Prescott himself committed Britain to save as a priority when he was environment secretary.

> **A derelict oil terminal beside a giant superstore in one of the unloveliest corners of Essex has been found to have more wildlife per square foot than any national nature reserve**

'Nowhere else in the UK has such a richness of nature,' said Mr Shardlow. 'It's ridiculously high quality. I cannot think of any site of this size which has such diversity.'

Bizarrely, natural scientists must thank an oil company with a long record of damaging rainforests in Latin America for the site. Occidental planned a huge oil terminal on Canvey Island and dredged up thousands of tons of silt from the Thames estuary, dumping it over old fields and grazing marshes.

They left the site unfinished but unpolluted when the global economy plummeted in the 1960s, but the myriad habitats that they created have acted as a magnet for wildlife. Meanwhile the kids who have used the site for bonfires and trail biking have unwittingly helped nature, too. By disturbing the ground, they have prevented trees taking over and created even more places for wildlife to survive.

'It's the combination of habitats that is so rare. There are very bare areas, basking places, short grasses, sallow scrub, coastal marginal areas, drought-prone areas, sand dunes, poor land, rich land. It's got bits of wetland, yet the whole is like the Mediterranean,' said Mr Shardlow.

But within a year, much of the site could be laid to concrete. The

East of England development agency (Eeda), one of nine regional develop-ment quangos set up by Mr Prescott, last year paid Safeway £1m for 27.5 hectares of the site, and commissioned environmental surveys. Before these have been completed, it has applied for, and been given, outline planning permission for 20 hectares of light industry.

Eeda says it can develop the site and protect the wildlife. 'We realised its ecological value from the start,' said a spokesman. 'But this is a key area of the Thames Gateway, and a national priority for regeneration. We are only going to develop 50 acres of the 68 acres and hope to convert the rest into a wildlife habitat.'

But English Nature, the government's statutory wildlife adviser, said Eeda's plans, as they stand, could irretrievably damage the site. 'It is a unique and expremely important site, but the 50 acres that they want to develop are the best for wildlife,' said Chris Gibson.

'Some parts of the site could be developed without much impact, but we think Eeda needs to take a broader perspective. There are significant areas of horticultural and agricultural land nearby which have no ecological value whatever.'

English Nature, which seldom gets involved with brownfield sites, said it is working with Eeda but is so convinced of the site's importance that it is prepared to fight to save it. 'It is a test case. There is a presumption in the plans for the Thames Gateway that brownfield sites should be developed. But they can have incredible value.'

The people of Canvey Island, long the butt of Essex jokes, are just beginning to appreciate that they have something unique. A campaign to save the site is starting, led by councillor Dave Blackwell, who said the government was preparing to destroy wildlife 'just for the sake of having a presence on Canvey Island'.

'If this site goes,' said Mr Shardlow, 'the whole government strategy to protect wildlife effectively goes, too. They would be failing to deliver on their own commitments. This is the jewel in the crown.'

Rare, very rare and once thought extinct

Shrill carder bee (Bombus sylvarum)
Once widespread in southern England, numbers of this bee have declined by 90% in 25 years and it is now known in only four areas. The Occidental site on Canvey Island holds the most important population of the bee in south-east England.

Weevil hunting wasp (Cercersis quinquefasciata)
A small, brightly coloured wasp that lives alone and collects weevils, which it feeds to its larvae. It needs open, bare soil in dry areas and nearly all its population is on brownfield sites in the Thames area.

'Canvey Island' ground beetle (Scybalicus oblongisculus)
The only member of its genus, this was last recorded almost 100 years ago. Rediscovered recently on the Occidental site, it could be Britain's next extinction if not protected.

Brown-banded carder bee (Bombus humilis)
Another bumblebee whose population has declined 90% in recent years due to losses of countryside flowers. One of the most beautiful in the UK.

Scarce emerald damsel fly (Lestes dryas)
This enigmatic damsel fly is restricted to coastal marches in Kent and Essex and one inland site. A very rare species, it breeds in shallow, sometimes salty coastal ditches and pools.

Plight of the disappearing butterflies

Butterflies are in decline with fewer being spotted in our gardens every year, it emerged yesterday.

The five most common British species – the large white, small white, red admiral, peacock and small tortoiseshell – are falling, particularly in the south of England.

But most at risk, according to a survey by the charity Butterfly Conservation, is the once-common wall brown, now found in just 10 per cent of gardens in the south and in only 20 per cent in the north.

Based on sightings in 33,000 gardens, the survey shows that butterfly populations are falling in the south due to loss of habitat and changing weather patterns.

Last year was the fourth warmest in 350 years, causing butterflies to migrate north in search of temperatures they are used to, the charity said.

'Some species are moving north and northern butterflies such as the Mountain Ringlet are moving to higher ground to find a cooler climate,' said Richard Fox, the charity's surveys manager.

'But once they reach the mountain summit there is nowhere left to go,' he said.

A spokesman for Butterfly Conservation, Europe's largest insect charity, said: 'The results confirm a worrying decline in many species and we are concerned that numbers seem to be falling faster in the south than in the north.'

He said that gardeners could help to encourage butterflies by planting buddleia, which provides nectar for adult butterflies, and food plants for the larvae such as nettles.

Vanishing wild flowers

How the flowers that once filled our fields are vanishing. Farming changes threaten a fifth of wild plants

Poppies, cornflowers and corn marigolds – they used to be a common and colourful sight growing among the crops in farmers' fields.

But now, along with such curiously named flowers as weasel's snout and shepherd's needle, these and many other once-widespread varieties are on the endangered list.

Conservation body English Nature warned yesterday that a fifth of Britain's wild plants were under threat.

And it said the chances of seeing them in the wild were growing slimmer by the year.

The flowers are being pushed out by increasingly efficient agricultural methods.

The way farmers grow crops has developed in the last 60 years and totally changed the picture of our countryside, according to English Nature.

Increased use of fertilisers and herbicides, development of more vigorous crop varieties, and the shift from spring-sown to autumn-sown crops have all had an adverse impact on the farmland flowers.

A guide to the rarest plant

By Tim Utton, Science Reporter

species, aimed at helping people recognise and conserve them, was launched yesterday by English Nature and WildGuides, a publishing organisation which supports conservation.

The guide, unveiled at Kew Gardens in South-West London, also includes farmland plants such as pheasant's eye, small alison and greater pignut alongside better-known native varieties.

> *A fifth of Britain's wild plants are under threat and the chances of seeing them in the wild are growing slimmer by the year*

Also detailed are the corn-cockle, small-flowered catchfly, spreading hedge-parsley and red-tipped cudweed.

Sir Martin Doughty, chairman of English Nature, said: 'The changes in the way we have grown crops over the last 60 years are completely altered the picture of our countryside.

'Before, we would have seen a glorious variety of colours across our arable farmland but now what we are more likely to see is a flat monotone.

'But this is far more serious than just aesthetic beauty.

'We have seriously affected the whole diversity of our countryside. The plight of farmland birds has been well documented but arable plants may have fared just as badly, if not worse. We need to ensure that agri-environment schemes take these species into account.'

The guidebook, *Arable Plants – A Field Guide*, contains information on more than 100 species of Britain's rare arable plants. It describes how they can be identified, where they can be found, when they flower and details on their habitat.

The guide was launched in an arable area at Kew as part of its Go Wild summer festival, which aims to spread the conservation message.

© The Daily Mail
July, 2003

Saving sparrows

Tony Whitehead discovers that Wildlife Explorers are helping to look after one of our most threatened bird species

Once, when your grandparents were as young as you are now, finding tree sparrows wasn't difficult. In spring and summer, you would look for old hedgerow trees, or around farm buildings. There, in holes, sparrows nested together in colonies, feeding themselves and their chicks on grubs and creepy-crawlies picked from the farmer's crops. In autumn and winter, the birds and their young moved out in flocks to surrounding fields, feeding on the weed seeds and grain left over from that year's harvest.

Going-going-gone

Today, sadly, tree sparrows are quite difficult to find. Hedgerows with their old trees have been removed to make way for bigger farm machinery. Farmers use chemicals to protect their crops that kill the tasty creepy-crawlies and weeds that tree sparrows feed on. With fewer places to nest and a shortage of food, the tree sparrow has been struggling to survive.

Nobody really noticed the tree sparrow's problems until a few years ago. After all, who would have thought that a humble sparrow could become a rare bird like an osprey or red kite? But, without places to nest and food to eat, they had become rare, along with many other farmland birds such as grey partridges and even skylarks.

Two years ago, tree sparrows had disappeared altogether from some counties. In other places, there were only a few colonies left. Something had to be done. But what? Bird experts from local bird clubs and the RSPB put their thinking caps on.

Tree houses

If tree sparrows needed holes to nest in, but there were not many old hedgerow trees, why not provide nestboxes? After all, a nestbox is just an artificial treehole. Across the UK, people hammered and drilled into wood. With the nestboxes made and in place, their makers waited. And their efforts were rewarded. The tree sparrows rather liked their new homes and moved in.

In North Fylde in Lancashire, the RSPB Wildlife Explorer group got involved in making nestboxes.

Nobody really noticed the tree sparrow's problems until a few years ago. After all, who would have thought that a humble sparrow could become a rare bird like an osprey or red kite?

They teamed up with their local high school and put boxes up at places where they knew tree sparrows lived. The sparrows liked the boxes so much that last year 74 were used and the birds raised an amazing 725 young.

Saving with seeds

But what about food? From their studies, bird experts knew what tree sparrows ate. They also knew that it was in wintertime that food was most important. It was during the cold months that the birds needed lots of seeds to help them to put on weight to keep warm.

The solution? Simple – put out seeds for the birds to eat. Not just a little bit like you or I might do on our bird tables. No, to keep the sparrows going, tons of seed would be needed! With the help of farmers in places where tree sparrows survived, conservationists set up special tree-sparrow feeding stations and kept these topped up with seed from autumn through to spring.

As with the nestboxes, this was really successful. In Wiltshire for instance, in the first year of putting seeds out at a handful of sites, the Wiltshire Ornithology Society found birds flocking to their new free lunches. And it wasn't just tree sparrows. Corn buntings, yellow-hammers and lots of other birds enjoyed the food too. The local birdwatchers even found a twite, a really unusual bird for Wiltshire.

All this work has been with the support of local farmers. It has made sure that the surviving tree sparrows are now doing quite well. In future, everybody is keen to work more with farmers across the country to show them how they can help the birds themselves by growing food in a wildlife-friendly way. Already many, many farmers are interested, and the future should be quite bright for the tree sparrow and all its farmland friends.

House sparrow
Female
- A mixture of browns and greys. No white cheek or black patches

Male
- White cheek without black patch
- Grey crown
- Very big black bib

Tree sparrow
- White cheek with black patch
- Brown crown
- Small black

- The above information is from the RSPB's web site which can be found at www.rspb.org.uk

© RSPB

UK a haven for traffickers of rare species

Report for WWF warns against lax laws and small fines. By John Vidal

British wildlife traffickers are smuggling in some of the world's most endangered animals knowing that there is little chance of being prosecuted and only a remote threat of being given prison sentences or substantial fines, an independent report suggests.

Britain is becoming an international centre for the illegal wildlife trade as a result of weak laws and magistrates' ignorance of the environmental impact that the traffickers are having on rare species, say university researchers commissioned by the WWF.

'There is an apparent lack of seriousness attached to wildlife trade offences', say the report's authors. 'The attitude of the UK's legal system is inconsistent and erratic, and does not reflect the impact of the crimes. The courts perceive wildlife crime as low priority although it is on the increase.'

In one case, the researchers found that magistrates only imposed a fine of £1,500 on a company which had imported £350,000 of shatoosh wool shawls made from the coats of the endangered Tibetan antelope. It was estimated that up to 1,000 animals had been killed to make the 138 shawls.

In another case a man caught selling three Lear's macaws was given an absolute discharge, even though fewer than 150 remain in the wild.

Wildlife crime is known to be increasing in Britain, with more than a million items found by Customs and Excise in the past four years. But, says the report, only 30 prosecutions have resulted from 2,211 known shipments of endangered animals during this period.

'The discrepancy is huge. Even the biggest seizures are not inevitably prosecuted. The largest 10 seizures only resulted in two cases', says the report.

Many crimes are not being investigated, say the authors, because offences under the control of trade in endangered species law which governs the trade within the UK of globally rare species are not arrestable.

However, people caught trading UK native rare species can be arrested under the Wildlife and Countryside Act 1981. 'It's bizarre that a person can be arrested for selling a common frog which is a protected UK species, but can't be arrested for selling a tiger or rhino – some of the world's rarest species. The law needs to be changed, giving it stiffer penalties and making offences arrestable to

> *Britain is becoming an international centre for the illegal wildlife trade as a result of weak laws and magistrates' ignorance*

help police stop this scandalous trade', says Francis Sullivan, WWF conservation director.

The report says that the police do not have resources to bring prosecutions, but suggests that this could be because the fines are so low and prosecutions so difficult to pursue that they do not bother. The authorities are thought to have problems in identifying endangered species and interpreting the legislation.

But other countries, the report says, have far more stringent laws than Britain. In Germany, wildlife traffickers can be jailed for 10 years for trading in certain species and fines in the US can be as high as £163,000. In Britain, only 49 smugglers have been fined a total of £50,720 in the past 15 years, and the average fine in the past four years has been £963, less than it was in 1987.

The report recommends that the government issues sentencing guidelines to raise the perception of the seriousness of the crimes among magistrates and judges.

In May 2002 the government said that powers of arrest for police officers and increased penalties for endangered species offences would be considered as part of the department's forthcoming review of the Control of Trade in Endangered Species (Enforcement) Regulations 1997.

Crimes against wildlife

- Shahtoosh, a fine wool from the fleece of the Tibetan antelope, can only be obtained by killing the animal. The antelope is on the critically endangered list. In 1997, UK police seized 138 shawls, valued at £353,000, from the Renaissance Corporation in London. Up to 1,000 animals would have been killed to make them, but the firm was fined just £1,500.
- There are thought to be fewer than 150 Lear's macaws left in the wild, and one breeding pair can change hands for £50,000. In 1998, Harold Sissen was prosecuted after three of the birds were found on his premises. He was sentenced to 30 months' prison, which was later reduced to 18 months, and also fined £5,000.
- In 1998 Wilfred Bull, while in prison for murder, tried to sell 120 rhino horns worth £2.88m. He was sentenced to 15 months and the horns were forfeited, but a later appeal accepted there was no proof he had bought them illegally and they were returned to him.
- Raymond Humphrey and others were found guilty in 1997 of collaborating to capture and smuggle dozens of rare birds of prey from Thailand. The birds were packed in plastic tubes and many died in transit. Humphrey was found guilty on 22 counts and given six years' jail, the most severe penalty yet imposed for wildlife offences.

© Guardian Newspapers Limited 2003

Wildlife crime

'Big time wildlife criminals to be tracked down by new unit'

Action to counter the organised multi-million pound wildlife crime trade and reduce the opportunities for offending will be the main role of the National Wildlife Crime Intelligence Unit, launched in April 2002 by Environment Minister Michael Meacher.

The new Unit, based within the National Criminal Intelligence Service, will concentrate on combating serious wildlife crime at both national and international levels. The Department for Environment, Food and Rural Affairs is contributing £440,000 towards the establishment of the Unit. Police Chief Constables are contributing a further £100,000. The new Unit will:

- Collect and analyse intelligence from a wide variety of sources and refine this into operational packages;
- Work closely with Police and Customs officers to take forward investigations and prosecutions;
- Identify the main individuals involved in serious wildlife crime;
- Gather intelligence in relation to priority species and related products e.g. caviar, ivory, shatoosh, parrots and birds of prey;
- Have access to police and other databases, as well as to sophisticated intelligence gathering systems and analysis techniques.

Speaking at the launch Mr Meacher said: 'I am convinced that the need for this Unit is greater now than ever before. Crimes against wildlife continue, pushing some of our most endangered species ever closer to extinction. And as the net closes in on these criminals, they find ever more sophisticated ways of evading detection. We need equally sophisticated techniques to make sure that we track down, prosecute and punish these "big time" criminals.

'In financial terms, some estimates have put the illegal wildlife trade as second only to the illegal drugs trade'

'These people will go to extraordinary lengths to get hold of wildlife specimens. We know that some specimens are collected to order. We also know that wildlife crimes are organised. There is also some evidence of links with other crimes, including drug trafficking.

'In financial terms, some estimates have put the illegal wildlife trade as second only to the illegal drugs trade. One estimate suggests that the global wildlife trade amounts to as much as 20 billion US dollars per year, with possibly a quarter of that being illegal. We are committed to combating this ugly crime and the National Wildlife Crime Intelligence Unit will give us an excellent opportunity to complement the work of the Police and HM Customs and Excise by tackling wildlife crime at the highest levels.'

The Countryside and Rights of Way Act 2000 introduced tough new enforcement measures aimed at combating crimes against native wildlife species in England and Wales, including increased penalties of fines of up to £5,000 or terms of imprisonment of up to six months for people found guilty of these offences. Police officers' powers have also been strengthened, with new powers of arrest and improved search warrant provisions also being introduced.

- The above information is from DEFRA's web site which can be found at www.defra.gov.uk

© Crown copyright

- Around 1.5 million species of animal have been named and described by scientists – and over a million of these are insects. (p. 01)

- It has been estimated that the total number of insect species alone could be around 30 million! (p. 01)

- The extinction of at least 500 species of animals has been caused by man, most of them in the last century. Today there are about 5,000 endangered animals and at least one species dies out every year. (p. 02)

- The tropical rainforest is the world's richest natural habitat. Over two-thirds of all the plant and animal species on earth live there. (p. 05)

- Using the data for 189 countries and territories, the authors calculated that the global percentage of threatened plants is between 22 and 47 per cent. (p. 07)

- BirdLife's latest research shows that a shocking 1,186 bird species (12% of the total or one in eight) are globally threatened with extinction. (p. 08)

- There are many causes of the current extinction crisis, but all of them stem from unsustainable management of the planet by humans. (p. 10)

- Almost 50 per cent of the tropical timber in international trade has been illegally logged. 1,000 globally threatened trees are threatened in part by unsustainable levels of felling. (p. 12)

- Climate change, ozone depletion, toxic pollution, noise pollution and overfishing have left the oceans in a crisis which threatens the future of whales and the entire marine ecosystem. (p. 14)

- Thresher sharks have declined by 80 per cent. Great white sharks, the predator in the film Jaws, have dropped by 79 per cent. (p. 15)

- Fifty years ago there were eight subspecies of tiger, but three are now extinct. Today, all five remaining subspecies are endangered. (p. 17)

- Over 800 species of animals and plants are currently banned from international trade and a further 30,000 strictly controlled by CITES and EU legislation including many corals, reptiles, orchids and cacti as well as tigers, rhinos, elephants and turtles. (p. 20)

- The illegal wildlife trade is almost as profitable as the illegal drug trade, and the risks and penalties for smugglers are much lower. (p. 22)

- The United States plays a major role in the wildlife trade, and is the world's largest consumer of live reptiles for the pet industry. In 2000 alone, at least 5.5 million live reptiles and amphibians were imported, with a reported value of 7.5 million dollars. (p. 22)

- The widespread and growing popularity of traditional medicine threatens the survival of tigers, rhinoceros, bears, seahorses and other endangered species. (p. 23)

- Around one in ten of all the world's bird species and a quarter of its mammals are officially listed as threatened with extinction. (p. 27)

- The numbers of many animal and plant species in Britain have declined in recent years due to the loss of the habitat in which they are usually found. (p. 28)

- In Britain we have lost over 100 species this century. (p. 28)

- In the last century, around 170 species of plants and animals became extinct in the UK, such as the mouse-eared bat, the Norfolk damselfly and the summer lady's tresses orchid. Many continue to decline at a rapid rate. (p. 30)

- England's otter population has risen fivefold since the low point of its decline in the late 1970s, said a report by the Environment Agency and the Wildlife Trusts in May 2003. (p. 33)

- Butterflies are in decline with fewer being spotted in our gardens every year, it emerged yesterday. The five most common British species – the large white, small white, red admiral, peacock and small tortoiseshell – are falling, particularly in the south of England. (p. 35)

- A fifth of Britain's wild plants are under threat and the chances of seeing them in the wild are growing slimmer by the year. (p. 36)

- Nobody really noticed the tree sparrow's problems until a few years ago. After all, who would have thought that a humble sparrow could become a rare bird like an osprey or red kite? (p. 37)

- British wildlife traffickers are smuggling in some of the world's most endangered animals knowing that there is little chance of being prosecuted and only a remote threat of being given prison sentences or substantial fines. (p. 38)

- In Germany, wildlife traffickers can be jailed for 10 years for trading in certain species and fines in the US can be as high as £163,000. In Britain, only 49 smugglers have been fined a total of £50,720 in the past 15 years, and the average fine in the past four years has been £963, less than it was in 1987. (p. 38)

- 'In financial terms, some estimates have put the illegal wildlife trade as second only to the illegal drugs trade'. (p. 39)

ADDITIONAL RESOURCES

You might like to contact the following organisations for further information. Due to the increasing cost of postage, many organisations cannot respond to enquiries unless they receive a stamped, addressed envelope.

Animal Aid
The Old Chapel, Bradford Street
Tonbridge, Kent, TN9 1AW
Tel: 01732 364546
Fax: 01732 366533
E-mail: info@animalaid.org.uk
Web site: www.animalaid.org.uk

Birdlife International
Wellbrook Court, Girton Road
Cambridge, CB3 0NA
Tel: 01223 277318
Fax: 01223 277200
E-mail: birdlife@birdlife.org.uk
Web site: www.birdlife.net

The Captive Animals' Protection Society
P O Box 573
Preston, PR1 9WW
Tel: 0845 3303911
Fax: 01384 456682
E-mail: info@captiveanimals.org
Web site: www.captiveanimals.org

Care for the Wild International (CFTWI)
The Granary, Tickfold Farm
Kingsfold, West Sussex, RH12 3SE
Tel: 01306 627900
Fax: 01306 627901
E-mail: info@careforthewild.com
Web site: www.careforthewild.com

Convention on International Trade in Endangered Species CITES
1/17 Temple Quay House
2 The Square, Temple Quay
Bristol, BS1 6EB
Tel: 0117 372 8749
Fax: 0117 372 8373
E-mail: cites_ukma@detr.gov.uk
Web site: www.ukcites.gov.uk

The Environment Agency
Rio House
Waterside Drive
Aztec West
Almondsbury
Bristol, BS12 4UD
Tel: 01454 624 400
Fax: 01454 624 409
Web site: www.environment-agency.gov.uk

Friends of the Earth (FOE)
26-28 Underwood Street
London, N1 7JQ
Tel: 020 7490 1555
Fax: 020 7490 0881
E-mail: info@foe.co.uk
Web site: www.foe.co.uk and www.foei.org

Greenpeace
Canonbury Villas
London, N1 2PN
Tel: 020 7865 8100
Fax: 020 7865 8200
E-mail: gn-info@uk.greenpeace.org
Web site: www.greenpeace.org.uk

International Fund for Animal Welfare Charitable Trust (IFAW)
87-90 Albert Embankment
London, SE1 7UD
Tel: 020 7587 6700
Fax: 020 7587 6720
E-mail: info@ifaw.org
Web site: www.ifaw.org

International Primate Protection League IPPL (UK)
Gilmore House
166 Gilmore Road
London, SE13 5AE
Tel: 020 8297 2129
Fax: 020 8297 2099
E-mail: enquiries@ippl-uk.org
Web site: www.ippl-uk.org

International Union for Conservation of Nature and Natural Resources (IUCN)
Rue Mauverney 28
1196- Gland
Switzerland
Tel: + 41 229 990000
Fax: + 41 229 990025
E-mail: mail@hq.iucn.org
Web site: www.iucn.org

Mammals Trust UK
15 Cloisters House
8 Battersea Park Road
London, SW8 4BG
Tel: 020 7498 5262
Fax: 020 7498 4459
E-mail: enquiries@mtuk.org
Web site: www.mtuk.org

People & the Planet
Suite 112, Spitfire Studios
63-71 Collier Street
London, N1 9BE
Tel: 020 7713 8108
Fax: 020 7713 8109
E-mail: planet21@totalise.co.uk
Web site: www.peopleandplanet.net

Royal Society for the Protection of Birds (RSPB)
Sixth Sense
The Lodge, Sandy
Bedfordshire, SG19 2DL
Tel: 01767 680551
Fax: 01767 692365
E-mail: education@rspb.org.uk
Web site: www.rspb.org.uk

United Nations Environmental Programme (UNEP)
C.P. 356, 1219 Châtelaine
Geneva, Switzerland
Tel: + 41 22 9799242
Fax: + 41 22 797 3464
E-mail: eisinfo@unep.org
Web site: www.unep.org

WWF-International
Avenue Mont Blanc
CH-1196 Gland
Switzerland
Tel: + 41 22 364 91 11
Fax: + 41 22 364 88 36
Web site: www.panda.org

WWF-UK
Panda House, Weyside Park
Catteshall Lane, Godalming
Surrey, GU7 1XR
Tel: 01483 426444
Fax: 01483 426409
Web site: www.wwf.org.uk

Young People's Trust for the Environment
8 Leapale Road
Guildford
Surrey, GU1 4JX
Tel: 01483 539600
Fax: 01483 301992
E-mail: info@yptenc.org.uk
Web site: www.yptenc.org.uk

INDEX

ACKNOWLEDGEMENTS

The publisher is grateful for permission to reproduce the following material.

While every care has been taken to trace and acknowledge copyright, the publisher tenders its apology for any accidental infringement or where copyright has proved untraceable. The publisher would be pleased to come to a suitable arrangement in any such case with the rightful owner.

Chapter One: The Worldwide Situation

Endangered animals of the world, © Young People's Trust for the Environment, *Endangered treasures*, © People & the Planet 200-2003, *Threatened species on the IUCN Red List*, © IUCN, *Return of the great white hunters*, © Guardian Newspapers Limited 2003, *Wonderful wildlife*, © Animal Aid, *Half of the world's plant species 'under threat'*, © Telegraph Group Limited, London 2003, *Globally threatened birds*, © BirdLife International, *Unprecedented extinction rate, and it's increasing*, © IUCN International Union for Conservation of Nature and Natural Resources, *The world's rarest mammals*, © Animal Info, *Disappearing forests*, © Friends of the Earth, *Threatened trees*, © UNEP World Conservation Monitoring Centre, *Whale watching*, © WWF-International, *Oceans in crisis*, © Greenpeace, *Shark numbers 'at point of no return'*, © Telegraph Group Limited, London 2003, *Trade in endangered species*, © Young People's Trust for the Environment, *Bushmeat*, © International Primate Protection League IPPL (UK), *Endangered species*, © Reproduced with the permission of the Metropolitan Police Service (MPS), *Advice for travellers*, © Convention on International Trade in Endangered Species (CITES), *Wildlife souvenirs*, © HM Customs and Excise, *The exotic pet trade and conservation*, © 2003 International Fund for Animal Welfare (IFAW), *Traditional medicine*, © 2003 International Fund for Animal Welfare (IFAW),

Current population status of tigers, © 2003 International Fund for Animal Welfare (IFAW), *Putting the con in conservation*, © The Captive Animals' Protection Society, *Red alert over rare species*, © Reed Business Information Ltd, *The 25 most endangered primates – 2002*, © UNEP-WCMC, *World must face up to loss of plant and animal species*, © The Royal Society.

Chapter Two: The UK Situation

British endangered species, © Care for the Wild International (CFTWI), *Endangered wildlife and habitats*, © The Environment Agency 2003, *Facts and figures*, © Crown copyright is reproduced with the permission of Her Majesty's Stationery Office, *Mammals facts*, © Mammals Trust UK, *Water vole numbers*, © Mammals Trust UK, *Otter numbers show five fold increase*, © Telegraph Group Limited, London 2003, *England's rainforest*, © Guardian Newspapers Limited 2003, *Plight of the disappearing butterflies*, © The Daily Mail, May 2003, *Vanishing wildflowers*, © The Daily Mail, May 2003, *Saving sparrows*, © RSPB, *UK a haven for traffickers of rare species*, © Guardian Newspapers Limited 2003, *Wildlife crime*, © Crown copyright is reproduced with the permission of Her Majesty's Stationery Office.

Photographs and illustrations:

Pages 1, 15, 22, 29, 38: Simon Kneebone; pages 7, 19, 24, 33: Bev Aisbett; pages 16, 27, 34, 36: Pumpkin House.

Craig Donnellan
Cambridge
January, 2004